PRAISE

EXIT STAGE RIGHT

"An essential guide for actors and performers transitioning into new careers."

— *Luke Crowe, Vice President, Backstage*

"If you are a performer who wants to make a career change and still maximize all your creative abilities, Ciara Pressler's *Exit Stage Right* is the book you are looking for. Written with insight, clarity and through personal experience, Ms. Pressler guides readers through the period of adjustment and toward a brighter horizon. Excellent!"

— *Brian O'Neil, author of Acting as a Business:*
Strategies for Success

"*Exit Stage Right* is the much-needed roadmap for actors exploring new career options. Ciara Pressler combines her firsthand experience with the principles of smart marketing to create a step-by-step process for performers ready to channel their focus and inspiration into finding a new, fulfilling role."

— *Dallas Travers, The Actors' Advocate & author of*
The Tao of Show Business

"For performers looking to redefine themselves and harness their creative talents for a new career path, the first step should be Ciara Pressler's *Exit Stage Right*. Ms. Pressler has a perfect combination of experience and savvy to guide the transitioning artist to a career that feels authentic, resonant, and ultimately satisfying."

— *Betsy Capes, Founder & President, Capes Coaching*

"Finally, there is a resource for actors looking to utilize their innate skill set and creativity *and* transition to another career path. *Exit Stage Right* will undoubtedly help those actors who have lost their performing passion regain a sense of artistic control over their lives. Thank you, Ciara Pressler, for honestly sharing your experience and insight, and for giving actors a sense of focus in moving forward to an unknown horizon."

– Jodie Bentley, Actor & Co-Founder, The Savvy Actor

"I always tell actors, 'The life of an actor is rarely easy... if you can see yourself being happy doing something else, you should do it!' Ciara draws upon her personal experience and marketing smarts to help performers determine if they need a new approach to their artistic life or a new career path altogether. This book will help artists create their professional destiny and step into a dream life."

– Darbi Worley, Creator & Host, Everything Acting Podcast

ExitStageRight.org

EXIT STAGE RIGHT

The Career Change Handbook for Performers

Ciara Pressler

[press★ler]
new york city

Published by Press LER New York City
First Printing, 2012

Cover Design by Annelise Pruitt
Author Photo by Noah Fecks

ISBN 978-0-9885135-0-1

www.ExitStageRight.org

To all the former performers.

Contents

Prelude

How I Went from Performer to Former

Everyone's final bow is different.

I had landed in New York City just months after graduating college on a tidal wave of optimism and unwavering belief in the lyrics of "New York, New York." If I could make it as an actor there, I could make it anywhere: My own sitcom in Hollywood! Shooting an Oscar-bound film in Paris! Commercials for luxury beauty brands in Tokyo! Returning to my beloved Broadway for a limited engagement! Reaching EGOT status was as vivid a dream as my peers' goals of middle management, marriage, and (what I viewed as) comparable mediocrity.

In my quest for performing success, I left no stone unturned. I inhaled classes: scene study, Shakespeare, Meisner, improv, auditioning, on-camera technique, hip hop, ballet, jazz, voice training, repertoire coaching. When I wasn't training, I was working on the business of The Business: mailings, headshots, websites, networking, casting director seminars, the entire career department at Drama Bookshop. I tried every approach I could find, accepted every role I was offered, created my own work, hired a career coach, all the while contemplating Hamlet's eternal question: to MFA or not to MFA?

Sound familiar?

And it was exhausting. Even with the brazen energy of an early 20-something, by my second summer in New York, while working a full-time day job and rehearsing four shows simultaneously (*Don't turn anything down! You never know!*), I had my first panic attack. I was performing at full capacity and expending all my creative and mental energy, yet my sprint was on a treadmill with no feeling of forward motion or tangible progress. I'd taken on too much, not out of career strategy or artistic passion, but out of fear of missing an opportunity. Ambition, when clutching my chest in its iron grip, became my captor instead of my motivator.

Eventually, even the idea of going to an audition began to make me nauseous. I started opting to work behind the scenes rather than take the stage. And after my last play in New York closed, I found myself back home in Oregon on my mom's sofa in a full-fledged quarterlife crisis. What was I doing – had I made a horrible mistake pursuing this as a career? The performer's lifestyle was not my dream anymore. Even if Spielberg himself had told me my big break would be next week, I was done.

After five years as an actor in New York, these were the things I was beginning to notice – the proverbial nails in my personal performance coffin:

Even A-list movie stars are unemployed most of the time. Very little time is spent actually acting.

Performing had never generated the income needed to cover my professional and personal expenses. I was usually working for free, and I was expected to do so.

Working actors weren't making anything close to a living wage: the median *annual* performing income for an Equity actor was around $7,000.

I did not have the dancing or singing chops to make it in musical theatre doing eight shows a week – and neither did most auditioners, even those who had been studying for 10+ years.

I wanted to live in New York, not relocate constantly for regional or touring shows.

I wanted weekends. I wanted health insurance. I wanted to go on vacation without worrying I'd miss The Call That Changes Everything.

I no longer felt connected to my artistic colleagues.

I didn't care much about what was going on in the industry.

In short, I'd lost my passion.

And so, for the second time in my professional life, I took a leap into the unknown. My circumstances were different, but they felt the same. I thought I was back to square one.

I soon discovered, however, that my years of experience in the performing arts would be invaluable for my next career chapter.

In retrospect, there are certainly things I could have done differently to experience more success and satisfaction in my acting career. While I did have the incredible fortune of a fairly formidable arsenal – enough talent, a versatile look, endless energy, mercifully flexible day jobs, and very supportive friends and family, I was pretty firmly in my own way well before I tried to take my place on the Great White one.

The turning point was when I let my frustration propel me to action. Reframing failure as learning who I had become and what I truly wanted proved pivotal to my career transition. As performers, we learn not to internalize a "no" as a rejection. We are merely gathering information – on what they could have done better, what makes casting directors respond, what material suits us, even what to eat for breakfast to perform at our personal best.

Failure is vital because it teaches you how to dust yourself off and try again. As cliché as it sounds, failure is one of the most important qualities for success, not just in the arts, but in life.

Persistence is also key and can certainly pay off. Taking a long-term view of your career as talent can radically change how you measure the day-to-day. But as the initial romantic spark fades and reality sets in, it becomes all too apparent that success doesn't come easily. When dreams downgrade from front row at the Academy Awards to front of the line at an Equity call, we're left wondering how we got here in the first place.

Fortunately, the months I spent reading every career book in print and doing real-life research on what I could possibly do next based on my experience, interests, desired lifestyle, and true passions paid off. Not only did I discover a new path that still ignites me daily, but also all the information I gathered, analyzed, and organized during that pivotal transition is yours in the chapters to come.

Act I

The Options

Some careers end gracefully; others leap into an unexpected sequel. The first step is to determine whether you need to:

1. Fix your performing career,
2. Develop a support career, or
3. Create an entirely new career.

Perhaps you're not as sure as I was. You've had some success and know there's more work for you around the corner. Your technique is solid, your network is strong, you know your strengths, and your resume gets progressively better. Maybe you have representation that pushes for you, or you've created your own work and have a loyal audience. But still, there's a growing dissatisfaction with the lifestyle of performing, with your particular career circumstances, or it's simply time for a change.

Perhaps you're afraid: you don't know what else you can do. Your degree is in music or theater or dance, you went to conservatory, or you convinced your parents that an MFA was a blue-chip investment. You can't let your friends and family down. You feel you've already invested too much time and money to back out. Or maybe you simply want different things than you did when you first decided to perform professionally.

No matter where you are in your decision process, you must be honest with yourself.

This book is not designed to lure you out of your artistic career. It is only a safe space to explore what your career means to you, what you want out of life, and how to go about getting it. You might even learn that you're already exactly where you're supposed to be. But the unexamined life isn't worth living, so it's time to shine a light on the why, the what, the when, and the how.

We'll start by looking at what might reignite your performance career – are you missing a crucial element that could be standing in the way of your success? Then we'll examine the value of a support career – could a better day job give you the financial and emotional stability that would be the perfect complement to your performance career? And if you're ready for the big transition, the majority of this book will map out how to gracefully exit your performing career and discover your next great role.

If you don't already have a pen and a notebook, grab one. Self-discovery exercises are on the way. Lists, glorious lists! But don't stop there – bookmark! Highlight! Jot down any ideas that come to you in the margins. Let this be your journal for getting to know yourself, both professionally and personally, *as you are right now.*

The best part of all? There are no wrong answers. You are allowed and encouraged to be as brutally honest as possible as you work through the ideas presented in the pages to come. You are allowed to be unsure. Play. Discover. Create.

What you are not allowed to do, however, is be ashamed of your experiences thus far. Chances are, any feelings of change resistance are just the remnant of how you expected everything to unfold. Life rarely turns out the way we expect – thank goodness! In fact, the black-and-white notion of "making it" may be the only thing that's hindering your current career. I became an actor to scratch the "What if?" itch, and I'm eternally grateful I did. Change is inevitable; the blessing is to be able to design your own life and prepare yourself for the best change possible.

So open your mind, be honest, and get ready to learn something new about who you are, what you want, and what might be next for your life, both professionally and personally. It's the best investment you can possibly make.

Ready? Here we go...

Entr'Acte

Is It Time for a Career Shift or a Career Change?

Every career has its ups and downs, and the performing arts are no exception. When it comes to an unpredictable career path, the arts take first place. Few industries have volatility as intricately woven into their DNA.

What other areas of business define as major events, we're familiar with as daily occurrences. Economic disaster? We never had financial security in the first place. Company closures leading to layoffs? Closing nights mean we get laid off constantly, only with no unemployment checks. Inconsistent income, few to zero benefits, low-paying jobs located in cities with the highest cost of living, high turnover, unsavory work environments, unbelievably demanding hours, even more demanding physical standards... The common assumption is that the hardest part of being a performer is rejection, but being told "no" is only the tip of the iceberg.

From constant coping strategies to temporary denial of reality, being an artist means accepting all of this as part of the lifestyle. On our best days, the life is romantic. On our worst, we seriously consider checking ourselves into a mental institution.

We've all heard the numbers. The average annual income for a member of the Screen Actors' Guild is under $13,000. Fewer than 15 percent of Actors' Equity members work during any given week. The median hourly wage for dancers is $13.16 with most dancers relying on unemployment compensation. In 2011, The U.S. Department of Labor projected the median hourly income for actors as a meager $16.20. Try living independently on the equivalent of a $34,000 salary in a major city and your lifestyle will be bohemian at best.

The National Endowment for the Arts reported that there are nearly two million professional artists in the U.S., and, as a segment of the workforce, they are more educated but less compensated. Surprisingly, for an industry that's regarded as progressive, women are still underrepresented. Dips in the economy are especially harsh on artists – unemployment rates rose twice as quickly during the recent recession than for the rest of the workforce.

In other words, it's not all in your head – the arts really are a harder path than most careers.

But you probably didn't get into this business for the money, or at least not for the security. You undoubtedly had an enviable combination of passion, ambition, and talent: a need to follow your dream that couldn't be ignored. These qualities, especially when nurtured with persistence, can take you a long way.

What we need to figure out first is whether you're at the end of this journey or simply need to re-chart your course. How do you know whether you're done or just stuck?

A career, in many ways, is like a long-term relationship. It's exciting at first, a blissful beginning where every new development is a thrill. But gradually, reality sets in, and your initially sexy lover now may not be the best lifelong match for the person you have become or want to be.

Falling out of love comes with many signs, some more obvious than others. First, a creeping suspicion, then actual manifestations, and finally, anything from a graceful exit to a total apocalypse. But let's avoid the drama and take the high road. Just because you're out of the honeymoon stage doesn't mean the romance can't be rekindled.

There are common overarching obstacles that can often be interpreted as exit signs. Only you can decide for sure whether your current frustrations are dealbreakers or challenges to surmount with creativity, determination, a little industry savvy, and a lot of self-reflection.

Even if you're ready to run screaming from your current career, pay attention: your obstacles have a funny way of resurfacing in your next endeavor. Just like making a conscious decision to stop continually dating the wrong type and start making healthier choices, being self-aware about your career obstacles can help you avoid making the same mistakes twice.

Career Clarity Questions

Do I Understand the Business of The Business?

Often, when artists go into panic mode, they take a craft class. But if you've already spent multiple years and many more dollars on private instruction, group performances, even a college degree, perhaps the problem isn't your performance technique but your business skills.

When you first dreamed of becoming a performer, you likely pictured yourself shining on stage or creating sheer brilliance in rehearsal, not drowning underneath a pile of agent-bound manila envelopes. Between the networking, self-promotion, auditioning, seeking representation, managing budgets, and the myriad details that go into the business side of being a performer, it often seems there's hardly time – or money – for cultivating your craft, let alone doing the work. Even if you have a degree in drama, dance, or music, chances are your school only gave a cursory once-over of how to navigate and build your career with intention and control.

The biggest problem with artists' training programs today, specifically with colleges and conservatories, is that they train artists in their art with little attention to the fact that they're sending thousands of entrepreneurs into the world each year. As a performer, you're CEO of You, Inc., which means you're responsible not only for creating and maintaining an excellent product, but also for selling it. Even if you have representation, it's you who ultimately has to call the shots and decide what your career will become.

Fortunately, many services now exist for artists who need career help: a business plan, a better-defined set of goals, financial structure, help with their marketing strategy, or perfecting the audition process.

"The commonplace thought is that if you focus on the business, you're selling out," says Jodie Bentley, co-founder of The Savvy Actor, a company that coaches stage and screen performers on turning their craft into a business. She and partner Kevin Urban, both working actors themselves, work with hundreds of people each year to get them un-stuck through learning the principles of business and marketing.

"Once you understand this is a business, you can take the personal out of it," says Kevin. "It's not that everyone is for or against *you*. Actors are trained to be all things to all people, but businesspeople have to be up front about what they have to *sell*. You have to be aware of your strengths, what you do really well."

Approaching your career like a business means building a case for the value of what you do as a long-term investment:

- What are your goals?
- What is your niche?
- Who is your target audience?
- Where is the market for your unique product?
- How much money does it take to get started and keep going?
- What investments do you need to make?

If the whole idea of art-as-business churns your stomach, perhaps you aren't cut out to tackle the realities of making a living as an artist. There's a difference between not selling out and simply not selling. To be in business, your product must be something people will buy.

Have I Defined My Goals?

Your career is like a road trip – it's impossible to lay out the route unless you've determined the destination. Sure, you have to be available to opportunities that arise, but being too flexible can result in career complacency which, in turn, can result in a sudden realization that years have passed with no real progress, just a few more lines on your resume.

Anyone can say they're a performer, but what does it mean to you to live it professionally? If you bounce from audition to class to workshop with negligible progress or artistic growth and quickly become dissatisfied, you might feel like you aren't moving forward. But how can you achieve success if you haven't defined what success means for you?

The lack of a clear-cut path to success in the arts is usually what makes the grass look so much greener on the other side of the career fence. From the outside, it seems like all you have to do is follow the [MCAT, med school, boards, residency, doctor!] path to be guaranteed a life of reliably escalating status and income. Unlike school, with a concrete structure of performance and advancement, careers rarely follow a predetermined route.

In this industry, there's a glut of talent compared to the jobs available. What will truly set you apart is making the decision to design your own career, be ambitious yet realistic, and map out the steps to get from here to there.

So how do you determine your goal? Start by brainstorming everything you could possibly want during your entire career, no holds barred. Spend at least 15 minutes writing these all down on paper. This is not based on what other people are doing. This is about what you truly want, and what will keep you in the game. Next, go back through and put a number after each goal you wrote down corresponding to how many years you think it might take to realistically reach each one: 1, 2, 5, 10, 20. Start by honing in on each one-year goal: is it specific? Is it doable? Are there definite concrete steps you could figure out to accomplish this? Do you have, or can you get, the resources you need to move closer to this goal?

Go deeper: what's the true desire behind your goals? Can they be more specific? Let's take a common one: Get Representation. It's time to cross-examine the witness:

- Is my real, underlying desire is to get more work, better-paying work, higher-quality work?

- Is an agent absolutely necessary to do this?
- What other steps could I take to get there?
- And if I do need an agent, who is this agent exactly?
- Am I best represented by a boutique agency or a large one?
- Would a manager be a better option for me?
- What's my timeline for getting representation?
- What are the actions I will take to get signed and when?

Be relentless. The more specific and honest you are about your goals, the more likely you are to take tangible steps to accomplish them.

Are My Goals Too Unfocused?

This one goes out to my Type-A (or type ADD) artists. You don't just have a goal; you have a whole spreadsheet full. You wake up with a new goal every morning and go to sleep with its revised version every night. You have a vision board and every self-improvement book and a subscription to O Magazine. To everyone else, you seem like a superhero. But stand still for one second: if you have ten things in ten ovens, something's bound to burn.

Is there such thing as too much ambition? Not necessarily. But there is a major obstacle in unfocused ambition. At some point it becomes not just pragmatic but also necessary to narrow your focus so that instead of running in circles, you're moving toward a finish line.

Also look at your longer-term strategy. Are your goals building upon one another, or are they scattered in every direction?

People with multi-goal syndrome tend to do the best with an outside accountability partner, such as a mentor or career coach. Those with no shortage of drive often thrive with a little external management.

Another cause of over-ambition is lack of clarity about what you really want. Are you running around trying to please your parents, impress your friends, outperform your peers? What are you trying to prove?

There is nothing more irresistible than someone who is clear about what they want and that unique, amazing thing they have to offer the world. Find that, focus on it, and let the other stuff melt away. You'll find success landing in your lap in no time.

Do I Need to Improve My Audition Technique?

You may be able to bring the house down with your on-stage performance, but what good is that if you can't get cast? Auditions are the main gateway to jobs, but if you're not showcasing the best of what you can bring to the table, you're doing the directors – and yourself – a disservice.

Auditioning is a separate skill from performing. It's common for coaches to try to extract the fear from a performer's pre-audition emotions by pronouncing that "Every audition is a mini performance!" when there's nothing performance-like about standing in line for two hours only to be cut off at your eighth bar.

Start to view auditions less as art and more as a technical skill. It's equal parts presentation, sales, marketing, and networking, not to mention that intangible, irresistible "it" quality we all want to bring inside the room.

Kathy Deitch, alumna of the original casts of *Wicked* and *Footloose* on Broadway, teaches audition technique for musical theatre in New York and for television musicals in Hollywood. Most of her students spent at least four years in the country's top musical theatre programs but find a disconnect once they finally get in the door to wail their best 16 bars.

"Actors tend to concentrate on the *what* – what they're singing, how the voice sounds – they're very preoccupied with having the right material," Kathy says. "People concentrate on all the wrong stuff – you have to practice the whole experience of auditioning. It's very different than the rehearsal process. You have to treat the whole situation like it's one chance. That's what you have to rehearse."

The best audition coaches often have experience casting – they have been behind the table for thousands of auditions and have begun to see common threads in what stands between a great performer and a great audition. Chances are you have the talent, but

in any given open call, a handful of tenors are hitting a high B-flat –
so what makes you stand out beyond training? Commit to mastering
the audition so that your unique, complete package shines every time
you walk into the room.

Am I in the Right Market?

You look great on camera! You are totally a sit-com type! Your
best work is done in 30-second bursts! Then what are you doing in
Indiana?

Different markets bring different opportunities. New York has
always been billed as the theatre capitol and Hollywood as the place
for those who want to work on-camera. But even that is shifting.
Many industry leaders argue that the true theatre lab is now Chicago.
Broadway performers have unprecedented opportunities in London,
Las Vegas, and even Sydney. Toronto and Vancouver have birthed
competitive film and television opportunities. There are innovative
modern dance companies based in the Middle East, and some
exciting new operas are debuting in Japan. And especially with the
explosion of webseries as a high-growth new market, content is being
produced everywhere. The New York/LA dichotomy no longer tells
the whole story.

Before you set up shop in a particular city, it's important to
understand that city's contribution to the industry. Is the work being
produced commercial or experimental? Do you need to be in a union
to work? Is your type in demand there, and, if it isn't, are you willing
and able to make the changes necessary to be marketable?

And it's not just the industry – you have to live there in between
jobs, too. Do you need California sunshine to feel happy, or do you
prefer four East Coast seasons in your year? Are you okay with a one-
industry town, or do you love the diversity of a global metropolis?
What's the cost of living? How do you like the dating pool? Do you
want to lay down roots and raise a family there?

Aida had been an actor in New York for ten years. Unrivaled in
passion for the theatre and the energy to constantly perform, train,
and network, she had a deep and wide contact list, and was tireless in
her dedication to her career and to the theatre and film communities,

organizing fundraisers, reading script submissions for the New York Fringe Festival, and taking every gig that came her way while proactively marketing herself to NYC casting directors. She was doing everything "right," but things just weren't clicking.

Resolved to try something totally different, she went on a one-month scouting trip to Los Angeles and decided to make a permanent move. Everything changed. Her training and work ethic were valued differently in a different market. She quickly secured representation and was sent on major auditions weekly. What's more, she felt happy and optimistic, as if a new chapter had begun.

Would Aida have done as well in L.A. if she had gone straight there out of college rather than spending her first professional decade in New York? Maybe not. A lot of your twenties – both professionally and personally – are spent getting to know yourself and what makes you uniquely you, which is imperative in this business. Not only did Aida's years in New York give her excellent training and a full resume to bring to LA, it gave her focus and the ability to ignore roles and productions that are simply not right for her.

Which brings us to…

Do I Know My Type?

As much as most artists dream of being the ultimate chameleon, no one can play every role. Fresh out of conservatory, where studying a wide range of material is of academic benefit, young artists often spread themselves too thin by targeting every conceivable opportunity instead of those that suit them best.

Even with stars, *especially* with stars – the most successful people find their sweet spot and corner the market, branching out once they've already established themselves as the last word in their specific niche. Witness: Julia Roberts, Robert DeNiro, Queen Latifah, Harry Connick Jr., Chris Rock, Anna Faris, John Leguizamo, Anne Hathaway, Angelina Jolie. And just think of all the constantly-working stars that are still playing nothing but a very narrow type.

So how do you determine your type or narrow it enough to focus your energy while keeping it wide enough to encounter plenty of opportunities for work?

It's not always intuitive – just because you're a soprano doesn't mean you can play – or want to play – the ingénue. Type is a combination of who you are and what you are drawn to.

Brad, a theatre major who had a very successful, 20-year career as a television news anchor before returning to acting in his forties, loved doing theater and dark comedy but quickly realized that where he was booking paid work was – you guessed it – by playing a news reporter. So he took the Law & Order and feature film gigs while building his comedic repertoire through indie projects until the two worlds merged to present his perfect role: satirical morning show host on the Onion News Network. Because Brad was able to be honest about how the industry perceived him as well as his skill set – all while keeping his sense of humor – he's been able to create a successful, balanced career.

Is an MFA Right for Me?

Hasn't every plateaued artist entertained the idea of an MFA? Being in school not only delivers the opportunity to actually perform, but it also provides a haven full of like-minded souls and people whose job it is to make sure you're a success. Is the lure really about developing your craft, or is it about postponing professional reality?

I would argue that graduate school is not the best option for most people. This is not a blanket indictment of higher education. But making a six-figure and three-year investment should be about much more than the illusion of security.

Before you even apply, it's time to analyze a few things:

Research the acceptance rates of MFA programs versus number of applicants. If you're not booking work now, what will be different about being "cast" in a highly-selective MFA program?

Write down, in black and white, how much each of your target schools will cost, including tuition, books, housing, and incidentals. Are you willing and able to take on this debt with no guarantee of working post-graduation?

Find out how many people in this year's class of your target school were offered representation within a month of their MFA showcase. Find out how many had paid work within three months. Do you like the stats?

Graduate school isn't just about talent. It's an academic endeavor, meant to build expertise in your field. Are you willing to do this work, or can you get the specific training and experience you need elsewhere – and for less time and money?

Realize that universities are businesses too. They have quotas, goals, and reputations to uphold – are you bringing them a complete package that's worth turning down thousands of other applicants?

The question to ask before you go to graduate school, whether MFA or MBA, before you commit to investing three years and tens of thousands of dollars, is this: What are the other ways I can get to where I want to be professionally? Maybe it's a matter of specific training, building your professional network, or goal-setting. A degree is not a guarantee.

Am I Being Realistic About Money?

Now let's look at your annual profit & loss statement, cashflow projections, and business development strategy for your performing career.

(Crickets.)

If you've never heard of such whimsical inventions as Excel and QuickBooks, if you leave all the money stuff to an accountant, or worse, if you ignore it altogether, it's high time you appointed yourself the Chief Financial Officer of your career to begin to clear the financial fog.

If you are committed to getting ahead of your financial situation, start by telling the truth: how much do you need to live the lifestyle you're comfortable with while having enough to spend on your craft, including classes, private coaches, audition wardrobe, photos, printing, postage, transportation, networking expenses, and covering stretches of unemployment?

There is an epidemic fear among artists about dealing with financial reality. Perhaps it stems from the impulse to build a resume by working for little or no pay, or a shortage mentality stemming from the gross imbalance of supply and demand of talent in the industry. This can manifest in many ways: living outside your means, drumming up debt, taking parts that don't pay, fear of negotiating your compensation, or even the lottery-ticket mentality of counting on a national commercial to make your year. But to be a responsible businessperson, you have to live in the now as well as planning for the future.

In the age of apps, it couldn't be easier to track what you spend and what you bring in. There's even performer-specific software to guide you step-by-step, assist with taxes, and see which jobs are literally worth your investment.

Give yourself a Suze Orman-style financial kick in the ass – especially with money, knowledge is power, and being honest about where you get it, where it's going, and how you manage it, is the path to security and success.

Am I In a Toxic Environment?

Let's bring it back to the heart: you're an artist. And artists need a particular environment in order to do their best work.

Are there certain seasons when your work flourishes – when you feel most creative, productive, inspired? Do you feel better equipped to do your work when you're on location, performing regionally, or on tour? Have you ever noticed that you audition better in certain studios? Physical environment can have a huge effect on your creative impulse.

It goes beyond artistic venues. Bartending toward the end of my acting career, I called the restaurant where I worked "Where Dreams Go to Die." Full of the most talented, personable, and damn good-looking people I'd ever met in New York, no one was doing much professionally. Out of at least 20 performers on staff, there were no more than 10 artistic projects that surfaced during that year, including my own. An apathetic atmosphere at a day job or in a social group can create a downward spiral: you're working late so you sleep in, you're stressed out so you eat or drink too much, you're making decent money so you spend it, then you're too exhausted to run your performing business. The perfect formula for career limbo.

One of the most strategic things you can do for your performance career is to work in another area of the industry. Performers have an ugly reputation for acting as if their jobs are the most important element of a production, however, having a wider perspective of everything it takes for a project to go from concept to creation can have a positive effect on your performance. You become easier to direct because you respect the journey of the director and creative team. Meanwhile, spending time in other areas of the industry builds your industry relationships, creating more opportunities for more work.

Avoiding Self-Sabotage

Isn't it ironic that often, when we get so close to getting what we want, we subconsciously steer ourselves in the opposite direction?

You sabotage your own success anytime you deceive yourself about how things really are. Any time you're avoiding, complaining, or otherwise pouting in the metaphorical corner, it's a fairly reliable sign that you are creating obstacles to conveniently let yourself off the hook from doing the work that needs to be done, and making your life harder in the process.

Are there habits you have, or identities you've assumed, that put you firmly in your own way? Perhaps you spend too much money so you have to work more hours at your day job, leaving little time for auditions. Or maybe you are surrounding yourself with people that pull you down, whether through negativity or their own career bad habits. And every single one of us has a vault of excuses not to hit the gym. But sometimes all it takes is a small shift in your repeat behaviors to spark a new perspective and fresh way of tackling things.

You don't have to look much further than the latest tabloid to find a rising star who repeatedly makes choices that make us want to slap our palms to our foreheads and swear, "If I had her career, I would never do that!" Instead, look in the mirror: there is probably something you are doing now that is throwing unnecessary roadblocks into your path to success.

In truth, every obstacle falls under this category, and not just in your career. An honest evaluation of the peaks and valleys in your life will likely result in the realization that 90% of what happens to you was, in fact, designed by you. The revered philosopher Pamela Anderson once said, "I am the common denominator in all my successes and all my failures." Begin by taking responsibility for your results now, and you'll find that your modus operandi will start syncing with what you truly want.

These Are Not Legit Obstacles

Notice that none of the above career blocks included:

- My agent sucks.
- The industry is too narrow-minded to see my true talent.
- I don't look like a supermodel.
- No one reviewed my last show.
- This industry isn't fair.
- My day job boss hates me.
- My roommate is annoying.
- The audition process sucks.

Can you see what these beliefs have in common? They are all rooted in others being the problem and you being powerless to change your reality.

Victim mentality is a choice that will neither be entertained nor useful in the pages to come. You started this book because you want to take an active role in designing your life. The temptation to blame everyone else is the easy way out. If you're going to be successful – at anything – the solution is to figure out what you do have, what you can do, and how it's all going to go down. It's in your hands, and you're about to receive the tools you need to make your life happen.

And a word on whining that the industry isn't fair. Breaking news: No industry is fair. But the fact is that we all have *some* advantage, at least one ace in our hand. So the goal is to play up what you've got going for you and exploit the hell out of it.

Whether it's time for you to find a complementary career or change directions altogether, this book is designed to give you a framework for finding your next great professional passion and securing a job that puts your talent to fantastic use.

The Point

★ A growing number of resources exist to help you navigate your performance career.

★ Take an honest inventory of what's holding your career back and whether you can do what it takes to fix it now.

★ Focus and resilience go a long way, whether in the performing arts or in your new career.

Support

The Advantage of a Second Career

Without exception, every performer I know who sustains a satisfying career also maintains a support career.

Sarah is a performer... as well as a real estate entrepreneur.

Stephen is a singer... as well as a web developer.

Drew is a dancer... as well as a webseries producer.

Dan is an actor... as well as a film producer and graphic novel author.

Chasten is a triple threat... as well as the founder of a multidisciplinary arts space.

All of them have successful, profitable performance careers while pursuing a second business that is equally important to them. They make a healthy living as performers, some in the six or seven figures. They have Broadway, network television, and feature film credits, and even a few gold statues to show for their work. So it's not about supplement – it's about keeping the creative spark lit between jobs, adding dimension to their lives, exploring other passions, and staying engaged between gigs.

It's Not About the Money

Without question, one of the most difficult parts of performance as a career is the lifestyle. Marked by instability, jobs change frequently, and along with new roles are changing colleagues, locations, hours, and demands. It takes tremendous focus to persist on a career path with so many ups, downs, and uncertainties.

Even if you're in a long-running show or a repertory company, returning to the same job for weeks or even years in a row, there can be downtime between seasons or tours. If you're ambitious enough to make it that far in the business, you may start bouncing off the walls after a couple of weeks without work. How will you keep your creative spark lit in the meantime?

Cultivating a complementary career can also provide a much-needed focus when jobs aren't forthcoming, or an opportunity to switch gears when you simply need a break. Performers are usually talented at much more than just performing, and have already cultivated the discipline necessary to learn new things and adapt to new challenges. Especially if you have created a niche as a performer, a second career can give you the opportunity to tap into the rest of your skill spectrum.

Of course, there are also pitfalls – being a performer requires keeping many plates spinning and you want to be sure that you have energy left after your other work to dedicate to your performing career. But complementary careers can feed each other – building momentum in one area of your life has a way of spilling over into your other pursuits.

Darbi took the become-a-performer leap later than most, moving to New York in her thirties after a lucrative sales career in Texas. She quickly built a name for herself as an actor, host, and voiceover artist, with a steadily increasing income to match her success. But Darbi isn't content to sit in audition rooms every day. Having grown up in a karate family, fitness has always been a big part of her life, so she built a second career as a fitness instructor. Her motivation isn't additional income; she thrives because she's a natural community builder with energy to spare. Inspiring others to be their best is something that fulfills her but doesn't always manifest in a voiceover gig. Her fitness career fuels her performance career because she gets the opportunity to use her entire range of talents.

Except When It's About the Money

There is something about the steadiness of a twice-monthly paycheck that eliminates stress from one's life. Knowing you have a steady stream of funds you can count on frees you to focus on the performing work you want to do, giving you the ability to consciously build your brand instead of taking any part that pays.

Creative professionals of all kinds balance their passion projects with their paycheck work. Writers, composers, graphic designers, chefs – all of these practical artists find they have to take jobs to pay the bills in order to pursue the work that they love most. Taking a job for money isn't selling out; it's being strategic. The trick is to make sure it supports you in ways that enable you to continue to work as a performer, whether that means income, health insurance, or a flexible schedule.

Identifying the right support career is a two-step process: figuring out the income you realistically need to supplement your artistic work, as we touched on in the previous chapter, and determining what you need out of a job, which is the focus of the rest of this book.

Working in the Industry

Working within arts and entertainment is the most natural fit for a support career. Rather than switching gears entirely, much of what you learn will be relevant to your life as a performer.

Having a well-rounded understanding of how a production comes together, finding its team and eventually its audience, helps you understand how you best fit into the business on stage or on camera.

Even if you perform full-time, I strongly recommend that you work or volunteer on a production in a different role. The awareness of how the creative team and crew work, as well as observing performers go through their process without worry about your own, will give you incredible perspective and make you a better colleague the next time you perform.

Learning another element of the business not only makes you a stronger performer, it will also build your contacts for future performance projects. Since industry people will be more likely to understand your needs as a performer, a flexible schedule and supportive environment may come with the job.

The trick is knowing when to wear which hat. When networking, referencing too many slashes can be confusing. If you introduce yourself as an Actor/Singer/Director/Producer/Fight Choreographer/Costume Designer/Key Grip, how will I remember you when I need someone to fill just one of those roles? The solution is to know your audience. Lead with what you want to be known for to that person, and then introduce your other professional pursuits when relevant.

Working Outside the Industry

If your day jobs thus far have given you diverse experience, or if you're finding that your interests and abilities extend beyond entertainment, it's an excellent incentive to explore work beyond the arts. Your choices are not limited to restaurant work and temping. If you find the right role and the right company, nearly any industry will benefit from the creativity and discipline you've cultivated as a performer.

Ideally, your support career will nourish a part of you that isn't fed by performing – it could be as small as an opportunity to interact with people outside of the industry, or as big as leveraging another major in college to continue a previous track. Being outside the bubble of The Business will also give you a wider perspective on how the arts fit into our society, culture, and individual experience.

If a potential retirement looms on the horizon, there's no time like the present to start investigating where you can begin to get the skills and experience necessary for another career. It doesn't have to be about finding the perfect job at first; allow yourself to investigate options based on what you enjoy and where you thrive. We'll dive into that discovery in the next section.

I'm fortunate that my day jobs while acting ended up providing a fantastic foundation for my current career. I took the jobs that were available and flexible at the time, not paying attention to any sort of logical career progression. But during my career transition period, I found ways to piece together my varied experience to build a cohesive narrative which gave employers confidence that I was a strong candidate. The third act of this book will show you how to do it too.

Taking a Break

Still, your performance career may need more of a pause than a few hours a day in another industry. When things aren't working, when you feel stuck, or when passion falters, a performance sabbatical might be just what the director ordered.

Four years into her career as a dancer, Erika made her exit. After performing in national touring companies, she transitioned to the administrative side of the arts, working as an off-Broadway general manager and settling into what felt like a more stable career. But seven years later, Erika dipped her toe back into the performing pool. What began as a few dance classes for fitness steadily snowballed into Career 2.0. Within her first two years back on the scene, Erika had top representation, booked the first national tour of *Rock of Ages*, and appeared alongside Beyoncé in a national L'Oreal commercial.

Erika will be the first to tell you that none of her newfound success could have been possible without a major change that led to pivotal life transformations and a complete spiritual shift in perspective about who she was, what she wanted, and how to go about getting it. Without these adjustments, living a fulfilling life as a performer would not have been possible for her. It took the space of leaving the business in order to fix what wasn't working in her art and in her life.

While the idea of leaving the business for a few months or even years seems scary, it might be the best way to reenter the business refreshed and refocused. The business will always be there. If you aren't booking now or have reached an irreversible burn-out, the bravest thing to do is to shelve the headshots for a while.

Your leave can be lifestyle-inspired as well. Maybe you missed that summer abroad in college and have a chance to travel, or you're ready to start a family and want to focus on your kids while they're young. Even though you may have lived your professional life to this point prioritizing performance above everything, some opportunities only come once – live a full, balanced life and you'll find it will serve your art.

A Word on Passion

There are a whole lot of people out there (and talk shows and magazines and, yes, self-help books) telling you to *Do! What! You're! Passionate! About!* – and that's lovely, inspiring even. After all, no one takes the leap to become a professional performer without incredible passion. But the follow-your-passion proverb can create an enormous amount of pressure. If your performance passion has faded, a lack-of-passion attack is only going to block you from discovering what's next.

Here's the thing: passion changes. What we loved to do when we were younger may have served us then, but a dynamic life involves growth and evolution. Does a wonderful, even life-defining early experience necessarily have to dictate your entire professional career?

Some passions simply don't translate to careers. Many people are passionate about being parents, but that certainly doesn't mean they must become professional nannies. What it may mean, however, is that their ideal job allows them to spend meaningful time with their kids, to make the money that will allow that time to be minimally stressful, and to be able to leave work at work so they can be fully present as parents.

You don't necessarily have to do what you love *professionally*. Your foremost passion does not have to be your entire career or how you spend every day. I know this goes against everything everyone has been telling you, especially if you're American, were born within ten years of the eighties, or have ever watched Oprah. If you love your children, does that mean you must be a stay-at-home dad? If you're crazy about tennis, will you be on the court at Wimbledon next year? Will someone ever abandon me on a yacht with only Rioja, Cheez-Its, and SVU reruns? (Please?) We have to dig deeper than the things that infatuate in order to discover those things that can give you a life you love.

Here's the other thing: passion develops. While turning your passion into your career definitely has its benefits, it may take some time to get there. Your first non-performing job may be a breath of recovery but not the exact thing you were always meant to do, and that's okay. Similarly, many people transform an ok job into a *wow!* job once they're in the door and figure out how to make it their own.

The inherent reasoning flaw in the "make your passion your career" notion is that not every passion is a sustainable career. The point is to get to the heart of why you are doing what you are doing, and be true to what you need to get out of your job in order to be a healthy, happy, well-functioning human being. There is nothing stopping you from infusing any job with passion, creativity, and perfection.

Recent studies show that the common thread between happy people of all walks of life isn't how much they like their jobs. It's the strength of their relationships. Knowing this, isn't it much more important that your career allows you the capacity to build the relationships that are meaningful to you? Or that the hours you spend at work are with coworkers whose company you enjoy?

Happiness is also a choice. Take pleasure in the little things, the unexpected moments, not just the standing ovations. Focus on the amazing experiences you've had as a performer, and be grateful for your incredible talent and drive. It really is true that attitude is what determines your experience, and you can choose to see your time of career transition as a dramatic horror story or as one that is exciting and full of potential.

Whether you continue as a performer or transition to a new career, understand that every job in every industry has pros and cons. And like performing, even the careers that seem the most glamorous on the outside have their own set of struggles once you get in. The point of this book is to discover which pros of a potential career are vital to your happiness, well-being, and success, which cons will destroy your will to live, and which things are just details that fall somewhere in between.

Career Change Support

Organizations and Communities

The need for career transition is nothing new in the performing arts. Fortunately, thousands of artists have successfully navigated this change, and several invaluable organizations exist to help performers create support careers or transition altogether.

The Actor's Fund is a New York-based organization working with performers from all backgrounds, including those in transition. The Actors' Fund Work Program (AWP) provides resources for performers seeking to change careers or, more often, to develop a parallel career that complements their life as a performer.

Available for free to performers who meet professional eligibility requirements, the AWP offers weekly in-person orientations and job search sessions at their offices in New York and Los Angeles, as well as one-on-one assistance from counseling to job placement. Visit their website at ActorsFund.org to browse free information on job options.

Aware of the special considerations regarding the longevity of a dance career, the arts service organization Career Transition for Dancers (CTFD) works with dancers as early as during college, encouraging them to begin to think about and cultivate additional professional interests. Their programs, also free, include career counseling, on-site seminars, scholarships and grants, and even support groups for newly-transitioned dancers.

"It's not one particular impetus," explains Executive Director Alex Dubé on the timing of transition. "It could be that your body wears out, your contract hasn't been renewed, or you've had enough of dancing. Injury, illness, how one has been treated in the workplace... Where a dance company launches a career, we will be there as a safety net."

CTFD's Lauren Gordon, a seasoned career counselor, recommends basing second-career exploration on existing skills and past passions: "The earlier you're able to plan or consider what you want out of your next career, it's going to lessen the degree of crisis. There's a certain amount of control everyone has in the situation when they're able to plan and prepare."

A program of St. Mary's College, Liberal Education for Arts Professionals (LEAP) is a bachelor's degree program for professional dancers that concentrates coursework into one day a week so dancers can complete their degree while performing. With programs in the Bay Area, Los Angeles, New York, and Las Vegas, dancers receive college credit for their experience as performers while pursuing new interests in the liberal arts. LEAP is led by Mark Baird, whose extensive dance career prepared him to develop a program that truly understands a dancer's needs.

"It used to be terrifying for dancers to think of the end of their careers," says Mark. "They feel unprepared because their intellect has been focused on movement instead of academic thinking. Being a college student gives them a second identity, giving them something to look forward to after their dance career, or even the inspiration to jump to their next career sooner."

The variety of careers pursued by former performers is unlimited. *Beyond Performance*, published annually as a supplement to *Dance Magazine*, is exclusively dedicated to telling the stories of dancers post-transition. Available online at DanceMagazine.com, its articles prove that performers are capable of jumping to a wide range of careers, from executives to entrepreneurs. "Dance is a somewhat short career," says Karen Hildebrand, the magazine's editor. "It's best to start planning for transition at an early age."

Especially if you are a dancer, there is a clear need to pay attention to your other interests so you can prepare mentally as well as tangibly for your transition. Instead of dreading your last days in the studio, you can reposition your first retirement as a gateway to the next thing you're excited to pursue.

One-on-One Resources

For the performers whose careers don't necessarily carry an early retirement clause, there's still room for self-exploration. Your type, talent, and physical ability change as you age, and you may find that leaving your career after your young ingénue days are over is the most graceful exit. Even if you don't meet the professional requirements for one of the above programs, working with a professional might give you the space to work through your career decision.

The career and life coaching industry has exploded in recent years, and options abound. A great coach can propel you past your blocks and help you see your circumstances clearly, with a tangible action plan to move you forward.

It's helpful to understand the difference between a career coach and a career consultant. A consultant evaluates your situation and gives you specific advice on what to do. A coach, however, follows your lead. By asking questions, making suggestions, and teaching you how to think, they partner with you on building a framework. If you're a self-driven person who loves Act II of this book, I highly recommend coaching. If you do better with the specific advice offered in Act III: The Strategy, a consultant is probably your best bet.

As in all things, do your research and comparison shop. What are the options available, what do you get for the investment, and what are your coach's qualifications? The unfortunate thing about the coaching movement is that it's unregulated – unlike psychology, no degree is required, thus anyone can hang a shingle and declare herself a coach. Ask for references, testimonials, or case studies of others who have been successful after working with the coach or the company.

Outside advice is always helpful, but sometimes change needs deeper attention than an action list. If you are constantly holding yourself back professionally and can't figure out why, it might be worth delving into the depths of your psychological motivations with a licensed professional. The great thing about therapy is that it's a safe place with an objective party who has put a lot of sheer hours of both study and practice into understanding the human brain and how it affects the way we behave and believe.

As with coaches, try to find a therapist who understands people like you and who comes recommended from a respected source. It's also worth doing a little of your own research on various psychological approaches, i.e., cognitive-behavioral therapy versus psychoanalytic therapy.

No one will ever know you better than you know yourself, so trust the path that seems the most true to who you are and how you understand the world around you.

The Point

★ A support career can provide you with the stability to make your performing career more successful.

★ Your career should support you emotionally as well as financially.

★ Many resources exist to help you discover, train for, and launch a support career.

Act II

The Discovery

Now that you have a clearer picture of your next career step, it's time to explore what you want in your life, both professionally and personally.

The first step in creating a new reality for yourself is to determine what you want that reality to be. By taking a 360-degree view of your life, you can cultivate a career that fulfills your needs not just financially, but emotionally and creatively as well.

Your career doesn't exist in a vacuum. The work you do affects who you are, from your personality to your relationships. The more conscious you are about what makes you thrive, the more likely you are to connect with your true talent and find satisfaction in your work.

Be deliberate in how you build your career – and your life. Deep knowledge of your strengths, skills, and what you have to offer the world will always benefit you, both immediately and over time.

It's thrilling to uncover gifts you never knew you possessed. Each of us has a unique combination of talents, abilities, and experiences. When focused, those qualities flourish, opening doors and connecting you with others who can benefit and build upon them. Doing the work is vital, but discovering the work that maximizes your capabilities comes first.

It's time to script the next act of your professional life. Rather than chasing the life you want, create it.

Vision

Creating Your New Career

Every part of who you are is affected by a potential career change. It delves into your identity and your expectations for yourself based on your experience, culture, and community. It can be stressful, frustrating, maddening, and anxiety-ridden. Some days, it will seem easier to just continue as you've been and give up on the work of change altogether. But the light at the end of the tunnel is bright, and it beckons.

Life is full of change, no matter what. Change falls into two categories: occasions where things change and we have to deal with it, and occasions when we decide it's time for a change and make it happen. Fortunately, this type of career change is the latter, so instead of feeling like a roller coaster passenger, appoint yourself to be the architect of the marvelous new life you're constructing.

The best news is: you've navigated change before! Whether it was going from elementary school to junior high, moving out of your parents' house, ending a relationship, welcoming a new family member, or just getting your hair cut, you've taken a risk and survived, just as you will in your career.

In other words: You got this.

It's time to get your creativity flowing. In the chapters that follow, we'll extract all your ideas, skills, dreams, nightmares, experience, contacts, and more. I promise you, the results will be impressive.

Before we begin, a note on brainstorming exercises. The first rule of brainstorming happens to be the same as the first rule of improvisation: always say yes. Don't question your idea, no matter how unreasonable it may seem at the moment, just put it out there. This isn't time to edit or judge… that comes later. It's time to expose every thought from every corner of your head and heart – you might be surprised at what appears.

Even if everything is not immediately cohesive, sometimes the point of self-discovery exercises is to define your thoughts, ideas, and feelings as they are now. The implications may not become clear right away, but five years from now, two jobs into your new career, you may look back at one of these lists and realize that you're in a position that captures everything you identified as your to-be-determined dream job. Writing things down has a way of creating clarity, if not immediately actionable steps. Any effort put into learning about yourself will come back to you in a positive way.

Grab a pen – let's go!

Vision Brainstorms

★ Occasions When I Have Successfully Dealt with Change

Take at least five minutes to write down every change that has happened in your life, from the biggest to the tiniest – we're talking everything from a divorce to a change in weekly subway service. Nothing's too small. Go!

Example:
My family moved to new state when I was in 7th grade – needing to make new friends led to me joining choir and discovering my love for singing.

★ Who I Am, No Matter What

These are the qualities that are an intrinsic part of who I am, that shine through no matter what I undertake.

Example:
I'm generous
I believe in equality
I'm creative
I work hard until a project is complete

★ The Worst That Could Happen

Nothing's more vicious than the voice inside your head that tells you that you can't. That you're not enough, you don't have enough, you can't do what others are doing. It's time to face that voice and examine what fears are getting in the way of you diving into your career change process wholeheartedly, with grounded optimism and self-compassion.

You are far more likely to discover what you are truly meant to do if you are acting out of love instead of fear.

Dig deep and list your fears about a new career path, and about going through the process of finding a new career. Leave some space between each line.

Example:
I'm afraid of going to that wedding and having to say I'm unemployed when I meet someone new.

It can be unnerving to see your fears in black and white, but acknowledging them is the first step to dissolving their power to block you from moving forward. So let's flip your fears upside down and create causes for motivation.

Go back through your list and write down ideas for how you would handle it if your fear came to pass. For example:

I'll go to the wedding and talk about the career I'm working toward if asked — maybe I will meet someone there who can give me great advice or who's in my target industry.

Doing this will help you see that it's almost impossible to be in a situation from which you couldn't recover.

★ The Best That Could Happen

Even better, think of how much your life and your circumstances could improve if you approach every encounter as an opportunity. The most successful people I know are opportunity-addicts: they've trained their brains to search for clues on the treasure map to their dream.

Brainstorm all the ways your life might improve once you're in your new career.

Example:
Easier to qualify for a mortgage
More time with my partner
Opportunity to travel

★ Things That Make Me Feel Motivated

The harder you work and the more time you spend pushing out of your comfort zone, the more you'll find a need for motivation. So next, list actions and experiences within your control that help you feel refreshed and optimistic.

Example:
Going to a yoga class
Listening to Hall & Oates
Reading articles on PositivityBlog.com

★ My Emotional Support Team

Just as important as what you do to motivate yourself is who you allow on this journey with you. Who are the people in your life that can carry that baton of belief for you when you need a breather?

These are the people you can call when you have a moment of doubt, need fresh ideas, need to vent, or just want a break from your career search process.

Just as important as the people you surround yourself with are the people you don't. Every one of us has that person – or people – in our lives that seem to love to point out what's wrong with anything and everything. The joy-killers who see the glass as perpetually half-empty usually aren't out to get you, but speaking and acting out of their own fears. Still, when you're feeling insecure, their thoughtless comments can easily permeate your subconscious and knock you off kilter. Scale back your interaction with these people as much as you possibly can during your career search process. Choose to be optimistic and focused.

Example
Amy – started her own business and is good at making new contacts
Aunt Bobee – said I could visit her for the weekend if I need a break

★ Rewarding Myself

Another great way to stay motivated is by rewarding yourself. You deserve it! The work of making a change is taxing mentally and emotionally. Rewards don't have to be complicated or credit-card kryptonite; they can simply be an experience you love or a lifestyle change you will be able to make once you settle into your new routine. Just make sure that your reward is something that truly lights you up and not based on what you think would be "appropriate." Then keep your eye on the prize.

This is what you will do for yourself to celebrate your first job on your new career path. Be specific and descriptive – paint the picture so you believe it and get excited about it!

Example
After my first month of stable income, I'm going to join the awesome gym I visited with a guest pass.
I'm going to draft a budget for a week-long trip to Mexico and start saving for my first (paid!) vacation.

Your Career Vision

Now let's put it all together and create the vision of where you're headed. Your vision is the big-picture stuff: how you feel, who you are, and who you are becoming. It doesn't worry about the how; it focuses on the emotional connection you will feel when you lock into a new chapter that is fulfilling and uniquely fit for you.

Example:
It is January 1, and I feel confident, inspired, and creative. I'm using my talents, including writing, interacting with new people, and being ultra-organized. I love that I have weekends off for the first time in my professional life and I can spend more time with my friends. I've worked through my fear and found opportunity in places I never thought possible. I'm rewarding myself by getting a pair of opera season tickets!

★ My New Career Vision

It is...

And I feel ...

I'm using my talents, including...

And I love that my life now includes ...

I've worked through my fears and found opportunity in unlikely places.

I'm rewarding myself by...

Revisit your vision as often as possible, especially when you are feeling discouraged. Just getting the feeling in your body of where you want to be will relax you and refocus your energy. Here are a few ways that my friends keep their goals front-of-mind:

- Print out your vision and hang it up where you'll see it daily.
- Memorize it and repeat it to yourself while meditating with deep, calm breaths.
- Create a collage of images that evoke the manifestation of your Vision.
- Share your Vision with someone you love and trust so they can hold it for you in confidence along your journey.

Go boldly forward! Honor the opportunity life has given you to create a new chapter for yourself by committing to the process and telling your fears that they're not invited to the party. With the new things you learn and new life you create, you'll inspire others with your courage – and inspire yourself with the new things you learn and the new life you create.

The Point

★ Life is constant change – embracing change is the key to becoming the architect of your life.

★ You've successfully navigated change before, and you can do it again.

★ Creating a compelling Career Vision will keep you focused on forward movement.

Lifestyle

What You Do Affects Who You Are

After years of the hustle, the performer's lifestyle can simply become unsustainable. Can my body take another season? Can I afford to produce my own album? Can I make it from West Hollywood to Santa Monica in 45 minutes? When it's good, it's exhilarating. When it's hectic, it's torture. And it's impossible to perform at your best when you feel stressed and overextended – both in art and in life.

Performers are professional jugglers of schedules and circumstances: constantly changing hours, a revolving door of colleagues, fluctuating finances, balancing second and even third jobs, and the need to be available at any time for an opportunity. Where others crave adventure, performers can find themselves craving stability.

It isn't just about now – what about your future? As you approach a given age or life stage, you may want to buy a home, live closer to your family, or travel more flexibly. You may find you want to be at your kids' performances more than your own. And that's okay. As we move through life, our priorities inevitably shift.

The single most important thing that should determine your job is the lifestyle you want to live. If your job turns you into a person you don't want to be, or conflicts with the things that truly matter to you, even a fat paycheck is not worth the true cost. It's time to get honest about what a particular career demands of your life.

What you do shapes who you are. Different careers and industries have personality stereotypes for a reason. While the essence of who we are can survive any situation, it only makes sense that the people you're around and actions you repeat daily become part of how you think and interact, whether at work or outside of it.

Our experiences affect us; this is good, this is life. So now, when you're at the fork in the road where you get to select your path, be aware of whether you want to forge ahead on a bike or in a BMW, and who you want along for the ride.

There are two lifestyle components of the career you choose: the lifestyle of the job itself and the lifestyle that the job allows you to have. One is probably more important to you than the other. For me (for now), my career is the higher priority, so it's important that what I have to do for my job is in alignment with what I want to do in general. But I certainly have friends who can push through a lot more career-related frustration because their job allows them fantastic compensation or more time with their kids. Either choice is fine; just be aware of what's most important to you.

Career Reality Checks

When I started out, I liked the idea of being An Actress. This is probably also why I changed majors several times in college – I could also envision myself as The Opera Singer, The Politician, The Whatever You Do With a European Studies Major. Luckily, I ended up supplementing my performing arts study with a degree in communication. We somehow end up where we were meant to be!

What I did not fully consider during school was the day-to-day reality of my first career path. Many of us were drawn to a major or a career in the performing arts because we so loved the hour spent in high school choir rehearsal that we wanted it to be our entire day. Little did we know that getting to the rehearsal stage in the professional world could mean even more hours auditioning, networking, doing mailings, taking classes, waiting in lines, and funding it all with side jobs. Actual performing can be a very small slice of a performer's activities.

The idea of a role or even a whole industry can be very different than its actual daily grind. A writer-turned-restaurateur friend calls it "fantasy versus reality" – in her case, the romance of being a writer wore off after her first book and the ensuing struggle to get it published, leaving her burned out and eager for a more controllable, less solitary challenge. It took a few years to crystallize, but now she owns and operates a popular bar in Brooklyn. And she absolutely loves it, even when the ice machine breaks or she has to deal with a neighbor's noise complaint. It's all part of the endeavor. It's a labor of love.

While we've all dreamed of careers that seem like a cakewalk compared to the performers' hustle, look before you leap into a Jekyll/Hyde career: attractive on the outside, but a monster once you get in. Every job has its pros and cons; selecting the right career track involves an awareness of the real lifestyle it brings as well as whether its demands are a personality match for you.

Pay attention not just to the job description but also to the actual lifestyle implications, from working overtime to the kind of people you'll have to interact with every day. Here are a few of my favorite career wolves in sheep's clothing:

Casting

The voyeuristic appeal of browsing headshots, the creative control of deciding who gets in, the revenge fantasy of being the one behind the table – when you want to stay in the industry, casting definitely has an allure. But being the middleman can range from boring to absurdly frustrating: you don't actually get to select who gets cast, that's up to the director and producer, and they can be tough and demanding customers. Add to this the after-hours hustle of networking seminars and seeing shows to find fresh talent, and you may be signing up for a two-job scenario.

Event Planning

Did you get married last year, and was it the best party ever? Did everyone *ooh* and *ahh* at your choice of coordinated cupcakes and custom cocktails? Then you should become a wedding planner, right?! Hold it: event planning is far less about throwing a party you'd want to attend, and all about pleasing the client with ridiculous attention to detail. The number of hours it takes to put together a seamless event is only outweighed by the emotional endurance it takes to manage high-stakes clients, from brides to businesspeople.

Law

Law has become the go-to opposite to the unstable life of a performer: a prescripted, lucrative, respected path. But especially in recent years, law has become almost as much of a gamble as being an artist – there's a glut of talent, often leaving only those with top-10 alma maters with the power to forge a lucrative career. On top of huge school costs, many JDs never end up in positions that allow them to practice law or to pay back those six-figure loans anytime soon.

Public Relations

While it's certainly a growth industry, PR is not all parties and hanging with celebrities. Entry-level positions pay peanuts, and are lot less about creativity, a lot more about busy work. If you get at frustrated when people don't return your calls or emails, and especially if you hate name-droppers, PR is probably not the path for you.

Starting Your Own _____

Entrepreneurship is not for the faint of heart. From Etsy to LLC, doing what you do is one thing, but running a business that does what you do is quite another. Nothing will make you face your strengths and weakness like being your own boss. Ideas are cheap; products people will pay for take a lot of work and smart structuring. Be very aware of the costs of being in business for yourself, from taxes to time to the tyranny of you being the one responsible – for everything.

Determining the Lifestyle You Want

Let's get real with questions that delve into your desired lifestyle. From the company you work for to the company you keep, your Career Vision will be supported by getting honest about what you need in order to do your best work and, ultimately, be happy. How will your career empower and shape your life?

Before you answer the questions that follow, it's also worth examining a *want* versus a *need*. What do you actually need for your life to work, and what's just a nice-to-have?

When it comes to regular time off, some people need two days off in a row in order to function well during the other five. For some, those two days need to be weekends so that they can spend time with family, or, even from just a practical standpoint, to save on child care costs. However, many of my friends love having a Sunday/Monday weekend because it allows them to have both a typical weekend day and a weekday that's convenient for errands, bank visits, and, admittedly, recovering from the fun that is being able to go out on a Sunday night.

Here's where it also helps to be honest about how much money you actually need to live comfortably. Sure, it would be nice to be able to afford to eat out at four-star restaurants five nights a week, but it's hardly a need. I am a huge cheerleader for daily exercise to improve health and happiness, but do you need a personal trainer? Costs like these add up. While you'll definitely want some financial flexibility, the idea is to keep your options open by knowing what you can accept as a comfortable starting salary and how that amount may or may not increase over the years. It's useful to start thinking now about salaries and other compensation like health insurance, paid time off, and retirement benefits.

Here are the factors to take into account when determining which careers will enable you to have the lifestyle that you find both rewarding and sustainable.

Lifestyle Brainstorms

★ People

Are you an extrovert or an introvert? Do you like discussing ideas or process? Since your coworkers can become a second family, be conscious of how you prefer to work and interact.

- What kind of people do I want to hang out with all day, every day?
- Do I want a workplace where people are similar to me, or is diversity of both background and talent important?
- Do I want a job that's social, or do I like to do my work in a solitary environment?
- Do I need everyone to be creative, or do I prefer to work with analytical people?
- Do I want to be part of a small team, or do I want to interact with lots of people?

★ Work Schedule

Your new career is going to consume a significant amount of your time. What do you want those hours to look like?

- Which hours of the day do you prefer to work? Does it matter?
- Which days of the week do you prefer to work? Does it matter?
- Do you want set hours, or do you prefer variety?
- Do you mind if people contact you outside of normal work hours?
- Do you mind working extra hours to finish a project or meet a deadline?

★ Personal Relationships

Ultimately, people should come first in your life. Pouring yourself into your job can be laudable, but not at the cost of the people who make life worth living.

- Do you prefer a social workplace, or do you want your personal life completely separate?
- Are you single? Do you want to meet potential partners through your job?
- Do you have a family, or do you plan to? How soon? Kids? How many?
- At what level do you want your family to live?
- Will you need to save enough money to put kids through college?
- Which non-work people and groups are an essential part of your life, and what kind of time do you need to maintain those relationships?

★ Money

We work to get paid, and how much we make determines the lifestyle we can have. Be honest with yourself about how and where you want to live.

- How much money do you need to make now to live at the level you want now?
- How much money will you need to make to live the way you want five, ten years from now?
- Do you need your job to give you status in a particular community?
- Do you care about living at a similar level to your family or friends?
- Are you in debt? What is your plan for paying that off?
- When do you want to retire? Are your savings on track?
- If you rely on a safety net or partner's income, will you be able to pay your bills if that source of income disappears?

★ Environment

Where you live is fundamental to your quality of life. Let's face it – the kind of life you'll live and person you'll become will vary if you live on the West Coast versus East Coast, city versus suburbs, in the United States versus abroad.

- Do you need or want to stay in the city where you currently live? If so, what types of jobs are there?
- Where do you want to live, and what types of jobs are there?
- Do you want to work in an office or in another environment?
- Do you do better work in a particular space – natural light, open offices, on-site?
- Do you want to end up near your extended family? How soon? What types of jobs are there?
- Do you have a partner whose job is tied to a certain place?

★ Sanity

Some jobs simply drive you crazy. Not everyone is cut out for every situation – know what you can handle and what makes you thrive.

- How many days off do you need each week?
- How long a commute can you handle? Drive, bike, walk, public transit?
- When do you want to retire and what will it take to make that possible?
- Are you willing to live wherever a job is, or is the place you live most important?
- Do you like systems and structure, or do you prefer a more fluid work environment?
- Are you good at managing stress? What types of situations are most stressful to you?

Now go back and rate each category – what's most important to you?

1. Put a star next to the lifestyle elements that are all-or-nothing, must-haves, can't-live-withouts.

2. Cross out the things you don't care too much about. Consider the rest and know they might play a role when making a final decision.

Transfer your list of starred items to a fresh page. This is now your Career Acid Test: when considering a job offer, this list can help you resist something initially appealing that could end up being your personal nightmare. For example, the prestige of working for an elected official might be attractive, but if fall's election season means your football season tickets are in jeopardy, will it seriously decrease your quality of life? Some jobs just aren't worth the sacrifice.

I encourage you to stay open and flexible. Be aware of what you need now and what you'll need eventually, then be willing to see it manifest in an unlikely place. A job that seems "just okay" at first but meets your basic needs could end up being more fantastic than you could have ever imagined.

The Point

★ The career you choose affects your lifestyle.

★ Start with your lifestyle needs to direct your attention to careers that support the life you want.

★ Prioritize your needs and wants to clarify your search.

Focus

Finding Your Professional Type

It's time to identify your strengths, talents, and abilities in order to determine what your next career might be. Where do you shine? When do you step up? In what areas are you inspired to work harder and push through to make progress where others might give up?

It's also time to admit what you can't do. By being in touch with your weaknesses — whether areas for improvement or situations where you simply don't do your best work — you'll save time and energy that you might have otherwise spent going down a path that isn't optimal for you.

Focusing your career journey is a lot like knowing your type as a performer — and just as critical to your success, stress levels, and self-navigation. If you play the rock violin, you can skip the Philharmonic auditions, but when you know that you slam-dunk auditions for athletic types, you'd better hustle to that Nike commercial casting.

Just as in professional performing, narrowing your focus to finding roles for which you're suited is simply good business. You have an edge when you highlight your strengths and seek the roles where others can best use your talents professionally. It's a better bet for both short- and long-term satisfaction.

Focus isn't limiting; it's liberating. Instead of infinite job postings to navigate, you can exhaust what's available in your priority areas, leaving no stone unturned. Instead of trying to understand every possible industry, you can research the fields most interesting to you. You can cultivate relationships with the contacts that stand to give you your next opportunity.

Compare it to the college application process. If you could do it over again, what would you do differently? Would you choose a major that required you to study abroad? Take more classes in different disciplines just for the sake of learning? Choose a school in a city you found more exciting?

This is your chance to start your next chapter with a focus grounded in *who you are* – with the benefit of wisdom that can only be gained through having been out there forging your own path in the real world. While you may not know your exact destination, giving the process some parameters will mean that you're more likely to end up in a place that suits and satisfies you.

Focus Brainstorms: Your Strengths

Welcome, my friend, to the fun part.

You've been focusing so hard for so long on trying to convince directors, choreographers, producers, casting directors, and the rest of the industry that you're talented, fantastic, and employable, that you may have forgotten all the reasons you're talented, fantastic, and employable. It's high time you remind yourself how amazing you are, what makes you unique, and everything excellent you have to offer.

These brainstorms will provide clues to your unique set of skills, preferences, and yes – maybe even non-performance passions. You may spot patterns, the same words or ideas recurring in different places. But best of all, these lists should give you a jolt of inspiration and optimism: there is so much you can do, and you are the one in control of deciding which direction you will take.

★ My Favorite Parts of My Career as a Performer

I may be a glutton for punishment, but I got a thrill out of the audition process for most of my performing career. My competitive side got a nice workout, and I liked the game of charming new contacts with what I had to offer. Now, I funnel that rush into the networking, new client meetings, and sales pitches I do for my own business. It helps me take the stress out of sales and make a game out of meeting people, writing proposals, and signing a new deal. Performing passions will empower your future career.

What are the parts of your performing career that you suspect you'll miss most after you transition?

Example:
Being in front of an audience
Working with a team
Auditioning

★ Things I Love To Do

What lights you up, motivates you, gets you out of bed in the morning, puts a smile on your face? Think beyond career-related activities.

Example:
Meet new people
Restore antiques
Update my website
Help friends shop for clothes
Discover new music

★ Things That Come Naturally To Me

The next step beyond what you love to do is identifying the things for which others depend on you. These are the things that trigger friends to text you or where you're at the top of their recommendation list. If people consistently rely on you to do certain tasks or for specific advice, it suggests a natural ability or a place where your skills have developed to the point of being very useful.

In ninth grade, my friend Ross moved halfway around the world to England. But for the first year he was away, we diligently kept in touch via epic six-page, handwritten letters that would take two weeks to cross the pond (yes, it was the olden times, before email...

but not before computers, don't ask me why we insisted on the ink approach). When a new letter from Ross would arrive, I'd tear into it immediately. Each one was terribly engaging, somewhat informative, but mostly hilarious with a touch of evolving Brit-inspired wit. We fell out of touch by the time we graduated high school, but last year I happened to glimpse Ross's name in the opening credits as a staff writer for one of the most popular (and clever) comedies on television. His natural talents have propelled him to a career that's an ideal fit – and now he continues to make me laugh two decades later.

The classic job-seekers' bible "What Color is Your Parachute?" is a confusing book without a lot of direct answers (but maybe that's the point). One interest-finding exercise it recommends is to identify which section of the Sunday paper you reach for first. When I did this exercise, my choice was a tie between Arts and Style. *Silly book!* I thought. *There's no job that combines those interests!* But lo and behold, just a few months later I found myself at an organization that nurtured emerging artists through high-profile events in music, film, visual art, and fashion. Even just having the awareness of areas where you crave more information or follow trends can help steer your ship for years to come.

Not just now, but throughout your life – what hobbies or activities, from massive to mundane, happen easily or repeatedly for you?

Example:
Languages
Mentoring younger people
Budgets/saving money

★ Areas Where Other People Think I'm Awesome

What job do you repeatedly get in your social circle? What type of advice do people seek from you? How do people introduce you? Maybe there's a reason everyone wants *you* on their fundraising committee: it's proof positive that you are reliable, connected, dedicated, and effective.

Example:
Coordinating a group
Editing something they wrote
"She always recommends the perfect restaurant"

Focus Brainstorms: Your Weaknesses

Now it's time to be honest about what you don't do well, don't enjoy, or where you are prone to fail. It can be uncomfortable to contemplate your weaknesses, but the clarity will help you avoid trying to be something you're simply not.

Dancers choose a primary focus early on, and their professional path tends to fall primarily into a specific category – ballet, jazz, modern, NBA halftime. Singers are limited by nature; their vocal type defines where they will find work. No lyric soprano in her right mind would walk into an audition and declare she could sing anything from Christina Aguilera to Giuseppe Verdi.

It's time to accept that there are certain things you cannot do, you cannot do well, or that no one in their right mind will pay you to do. Rather than terrifying, this notion should be remarkably freeing. No more staying up all night to find a belt-mix, 16-bar ballad to showcase the high E you might be able to hit on a good day after a gallon of chamomile and a shot of brandy. Instead, you can get a full eight hours of sleep knowing no one will ask you to pirouette if you're really a jazz hands kinda guy.

Most promisingly, there may be interests you're willing to cultivate in order to broaden your skill set and position yourself for a new field.

★ Things I Hate To Do

What tasks or types of tasks do you dread? What do you have a hard time doing or finishing? Where have you folded your cards or gotten stuck in past projects – or opted out altogether?

Example:
Work without direction

Travel for business
Deal with bureaucracy

★ Areas Where I'm Prone to Fail

I know. It's not fun to reflect on the negatives, but as any successful person will tell you, failures can be signposts pointing you in a different direction. By identifying areas where you repeatedly fall short, give up, or cop out, you'll get a strong reading of where you might do better to try something completely different.

When has something just not worked out? When have you been fired or quit? When does motivation completely elude you?

Example:
In teams/companies without a clear hierarchy
When I'm not financially rewarded for performing better than others
When I'm not intellectually challenged

★ What I Don't Want

Know thyself: be honest about what you know you simply don't want for your career or your life.

Example:
Income ceiling
To live in a small town
Overly political environment

★ Things I Might Like to Improve or Learn

Maybe you're not an expert – yet. If given the opportunity, are there areas for improvement where you'd relish cultivating a new skill set?

What continually grabs your attention? Which non-performance industries pique your interest? Are you part of any networks, on any mailing lists, that might indicate an impetus toward a new career or industry?

Example:
Volunteering at the elementary school in my neighborhood
NPR junkie
Learning new effects in Photoshop

Researching Your Interests

You may be lucky in that you have hidden talents or established skills that will be useful for pursuing non-performance careers, or even industries beyond entertainment. Perhaps a day job gave you administrative skills or exposure to another industry.

I was fortunate that during my years as an actor I had day jobs in both tech and finance – excellent resume builders as well as opportunities to acquire skills and learn how to conduct myself in an office environment. Later on, I filled in income gaps by waiting tables, bartending, and intermittent freelance gigs in event-based brand promotion, which propelled my resume toward a career in marketing.

However, my interest in politics kept popping up in my various "what do I love?" lists. My career transition happened to coincide with a local election year, so I volunteered on four campaigns and even interned for a member of Congress. These additional activities not only gave me something to look forward to in between days of sending out resumes – they showed me that I preferred politics as a community member, not an employee, saving me a third career transition down the line (knock on wood).

Researching potential careers is fun – it's an opportunity to be creative, build your contact list, and try on different jobs for size. If you can find the time and target the opportunity, I highly recommend a short-term internship or freelance engagement to experiment with a new field. But there's more than one way to find out about different industries, even if you're afraid of commitment:

- Volunteering
- Internships

- Informational interviews
- Job boards
- Free seminars at graduate schools
- Online courses
- Freelance work
- Host committees
- Industry networking events
- Conferences
- Industry magazines and newsletters

The best-case outcome of your research will be finding out whether you still want to pursue a given direction. It's okay to realize that a particular industry isn't a professional fit, or that you have to take some classes in order to have a realistic shot.

A position doesn't have to be available in order for you to fill it. Create your own opportunities. If you love a certain charity, ask if they need help at their next fundraising event. Offer to intern one day a week at a company where you have a contact. Take your friend to coffee and ask her all about how she got into her current job. You'll be surprised how much people love to help.

My career transition story came full circle last spring in an interesting way. An actor applied to my internship program with a beautifully-written letter explaining that she was researching alternate career paths after a frustrating acting year. Not only was she a perfect fit for my company's needs, she read the first draft of this book, giving me valuable suggestions to make it better. And ultimately, a career change wasn't needed – just two weeks after her internship ended, she booked her Broadway debut. But spending time investigating a new career path gave her confidence that she could be successful in another field and helped her understand what she wanted to get out of her career as a performer.

A lot of the traits and preferences you are discovering here may not seem readily translatable to a particular job. But narrowing your focus and putting things in writing has a way of sneaking into your subconscious, subtly directing your actions and steering your job search ship. Sometimes it's not until you get to an unexpected destination that you realize you're exactly where you were always supposed to be.

The Point

★You're much likelier to be successful if you are doing something that suits your strengths.

★Explore where your natural proclivities intersect with tangible career skills.

★Research real-world careers to learn about and create opportunities.

Act III

The Strategy

Due to the current pace of technology, any step by step, how-to job search book will be outdated within the year. Rather than focus on details, let's look at the big picture of how to decide and discover what to do in your job search.

This is not only about how to package yourself, but how to go for what you want – the truths of which are not dependent on the individual tactic, which will inevitably vary by individual, location, and what resources are available to you.

The absence of five-step plans, specific roadmaps, and timelines may be frustrating, but a cookie-cutter guide that wants you to take the same approach as everyone else in your job market isn't going to serve you well in the long run. Instead, take responsibility for your own career destiny, and continue the development of your own unique approach to your lifelong career path.

We're all familiar with the proverb "Lead a man to fish, and he'll eat for a day; teach a man to fish, and he'll eat forever." The Strategy gives you the fundamentals of figuring out your own process and building custom action steps based on your unique goal.

I don't want you to become dependent. I want you to be independent. Strategic. Smart. Creative. It's more challenging terrain than simply following a map, but it will set you up for greater success and satisfaction.

The next few chapters will give you tangible, actionable advice, but the main focus is teaching you how to think strategically about positioning yourself as an ideal job candidate and how to use your performing background to your advantage.

Resume

Identifying the Value of Your Experience

I once read an article in The New York Times that astutely pointed out that drug dealing could viably be considered an excellent resume builder. What company wouldn't consider a candidate whose skill set includes:

- *Sales professional with high client retention rate*
- *Able to work in a high-stakes environment under deadline*
- *Result-oriented communication skills*
- *Comfortable working unconventional hours*
- *Consistent management of high-turnover workforce*
- *Able to communicate effectively with volatile customers*
- *Track record of parlaying professional experience to parallel career (ref: Rap Lyricist)*

In other words, if dealing drugs can be put into a business-friendly bulleted resume item, so can performing arts experience.

The most important thing you can learn here is how to position yourself for your target audience. Rather than assume you don't fit perfectly into what they're looking for, build a case as to why you are the ideal candidate to solve their problem. The resume is your opportunity to break down why the professional experience you've had until now is relevant and valuable.

What we are not doing is "improving the truth." Resume lies will inevitably catch up with you, and they're simply not necessary when you approach your experience and skills thoughtfully. The name of the game is honesty and transparency. Smart employers will be interested in someone who can succinctly summarize their experience, why their goals have shifted, and what they can bring to the table.

Performing incorporates any number of skills that can be transferred to a completely different professional scenario. Beyond performing, if you have ever produced a show, taught a class, worked on set, or aided with another element of a production, you have unique skills that could greatly benefit the right company. If you have had day jobs, however varied, each gave you an experience that built your value as a worker. I invite you to explore the ways your wide – or narrow – job experience thus far can creatively meld into a unique, personalized narrative.

I am also asking you to partner with me to make performance a viable paragraph in the experience section of your resume. "I used to be a… " should not be a skeleton in your closet, it should be a flag in your front yard. If we could look at all the ways the arts have positively shaped us with a critical, professional eye, and learn how to communicate this to those outside the industry, the arts would be programmed and funded faster than you could say "new stadium."

In fact, let's compare the arts to sports, insofar as the skills honed both translate to other careers – and to life.

Sports	Arts
▪ *Teamwork*	▪ *Teamwork*
▪ *Discipline*	▪ *Discipline*
▪ *High-pressure situations*	▪ *High-pressure situations*
▪ *Ability to present in front of an audience*	▪ *Ability to present in front of an audience*
▪ *Being prepared for a hard deadline*	▪ *Being prepared for a hard deadline*

You get the point.

Begin by thinking about the wider categories of your job as a performer. Being an actor, singer, musician, or dancer is not just standing on stage interpreting someone else's material. You played job functions as an artist-preneur that went beyond the stage in development, auditioning, administration, finance, and beyond. Where did you thrive in each of these areas?

Example:

June 2004 – August 2012
Performer, Multiple Productions
- Performed in over 30 productions, including Sundance Award-winning film
- Comprehensive tracking of professional budget, schedules, contacts, and engagements
- Ability to memorize material and perform on demand
- Recognized for strength in adapting quickly when joining existing companies

Creating a Kick-Ass Resume

Resumes should be simple, clear, and to the point. Very rarely will the first evaluator pore over every line of your resume. Since they are going to scan it for keywords, you should fill it with the ones that will stand out and stick.

Usually, your resume should be one page, total. If you're spilling into two, or *gasp!* three pages, chances are slim that the additional pages are being read, and chances are obese that you're over-embellishing.

Resumes should never, ever, contain a single spelling or grammar error. Even if you were a fourth grade spelling champion, or played one in *The 25th Annual Putnam County Spelling Bee*, have someone very smart and very particular proofread it for you.

The biggest and boldest thing on your resume should be your name. After that, all other text can stay the same size. If you're going to vary it, be consistent: make *all* the section headers bold or *all* your contact information in caps. Confuse the eye, confuse the reader.

Resumes must be easy on the eyes and never too busy. Use a basic, readable font. No frivolous images. No stationery. No background color. No graphics or photo, unless you have a clear, industry-specific reason.

Resume Elements

Contact Information

The easiest part – and here is the great news: you no longer have to quantify your body or voice type! The header of your resume only needs your name and contact information. Never include your social security number or date of birth.

It's customary to include your physical address, if only to prove that you live in the area where the job is located. If privacy is a concern, or you need a chance to explain your commute or relocation plans, forego the address and include your phone and email address.

Your email address absolutely must be very close to the format [firstnamelastname {at} gmail.com]. Even email addresses can be a point of judgment depending on your audience: some companies, especially in the tech field, delete applicants with Hotmail or Yahoo addresses, with Gmail being the acceptable standard – unless you use your custom domain name (me@myname.com). Definitely avoid anything that could potentially be viewed as cute (shoefreak87@me.com), immature (omega4ever@almamater.edu), or outside the industry you're applying for (benthetenor@aol.com).

Objective

The objective is one or two brief, specific sentences that explain the type of role you want and the type of company for which you want to work. It's nonfiction, a place to get to the point without revealing too much or getting too cutesy.

Tempting but inappropriate objective lines include:

Seeking to parlay my singing experience into running a multi-million dollar recording studio empire. (Too ambitious.)

To contribute my talents and skills to a growing company or organization in a challenging and rewarding way through diverse projects. (Too broad.)

Pretty much anything as long as it pays at least $60K with full benefits and I don't have to work weekends. (Too honest.)

Personally, I'm not a fan of the objective section of the resume. It risks being too vague if not tailored to each application, but with the opposite risk of being too pandering if it *is* tailored to each application. Clearly, the objective is to get an offer for the position for which you're applying – any elaboration on why can go in your cover letter. I have always left the objective out altogether. But if you're hurting for space or want to reiterate your personal job search mission, definitely include a well-written, specific objective.

Better objective sentences include:

Seeking an entry-level role in the medical industry with opportunity for growth.

To secure a position with Supreme, Inc., in product development.

Join the Warby Parker Customer Service team to expand my experience in client relations and social media.

Experience

Unlike the performer's resume which lists each project on just one line, a professional resume begs for more elaboration. Isn't that great? Instead of reducing a year of work to just one line, you can highlight your accomplishments, what made the experience significant, and, more importantly, shape the viewer's perception of what that role was all about.

The must-includes in your experience section are company, role, dates employed, and role description. The format can vary – bulleted lists versus paragraph – but keep it easy to read, as brief as possible, and full of hard-hitting keywords.

Here's an example of how a performer's experience can go from confusing to tantalizing:

Before

9/2002 – 6/2003   **Performer, Instructor**
Freestyle Repertory Theatre, New York City
Ensemble member and teaching artist for New York City's professional improvisational theatre company. Performances included daily and weekly in schools and in Manhattan's theatre district. Teaching residencies included work with students of all ages and backgrounds. Demonstrated ability to be creative and interact with anyone immediately and effectively.

After

9/2002 – 6/2003   **Freestyle Repertory Theatre, New York City**
Artist-in-Residence, Company Member
- Daily live performances for audiences of 50 – 500 throughout Tri-State area.
- Multiple weekly teaching residencies in New York City public schools.
- Development of teaching curricula and event structure in team environment.

Both contain the all-important keywords that are the anchors of your resume. But bullets are simply easier to read and urge you get to the point while insisting you narrow down to just the most important points. Leave the embellished descriptions to your intro letter.

Resume Considerations

Do I have to include dates? A lot of my day jobs were three-month stints.

Yes, you must include dates, but if you have had a lot of gigs with a common theme, such as the same type of freelance work, you can group them under a common heading (i.e., Arts Administration Internships) to make yourself look experienced instead of cut-and-run.

Do I have to list every job?

No. Some jobs are too brief, irrelevant, or redundant. Every word on your resume should bring fresh or evolving information. Don't repeat yourself.

I removed restaurant work from my professional resume because I couldn't make it fit the career story I wanted to tell and I had enough other experience to fill the page – it's fine to do the same if it makes sense for you.

How many bullets should I have under each job?

No less than two, no more than five. The most recent or relevant job should have the most; and vice versa. If you only have one or two jobs for your resume, you can increase bullets, grouping by function or category.

What if a job was unpaid?

It's still possible that a volunteer position could make your resume stronger. Here are some guiding principles:

- Was it a role for which others are normally paid?
- Did it require skills or experiences that you want to highlight?
- Did it last for an extended period of time?
- Does it account for a gap in your resume?
- Did the role evolve or were you promoted to more responsibility?

If you have any major gaps or overlaps in your job history, you must explain why. This is a great thing to include in your cover letter and to elaborate in your interview.

Internships & Volunteering

Related experience can be pivotal for a resume that is otherwise lacking in relevant roles. If an internship or extended volunteer engagement gave you relevant skills for your new career direction, by all means, include them in their own section. You can also include these experiences as a relevant bullet point under Experience or Education.

Education

The only thing that absolutely must be here is the name of your college. Optional additions are your degree, year of graduation, and notable accomplishments while in school, but if any of these undermine your job goals, I give you permission to leave these details off. Break the rules when it serves you.

Do not include your high school. Do not include honors that are not that big of a deal. Do not include clubs and long-past affiliations: this is a professional application, not a college one. Again, it's better to keep it simple and strong than to stuff it with fluff.

Before

Class of 1994, Sunset University
B.A. Music, Emphasis in Music History
- Dean's List, 3 semesters
- Alpha Alpha Alpha pledge
- Summer abroad in England
- Asian American Student League

After

Westview College *Bachelor's Degree*
- Graduated Magna Cum Laude
- Sole Recipient of The Natasha Joyce Vocal Music Scholarship
- Administrative Volunteer for Children's Fund of Montana

Skills

Skills are an optional category to enhance experience with concrete things you can do, from photo editing to presentational speaking. As with performing, do not list skills you don't have. Any skills you list must be relevant to the job, and you must be at least moderately proficient. Don't list web design if you've only filled out website templates; don't list Spanish if you only took two years in high school. A brief resume that is strong and sincere is best.

Tricks of Your Trade

The look and feel of your resume communicates who you are and if you "get it." Resumes are the key piece of marketing literature for the package you're selling, and as such, should incorporate some key nonverbal cues to communicate who you are and why you're the right fit for the job. You can't ignore details like font, colors, format, length, and even logo if you want to stand out in today's market. Let your target industry be your guide.

Fonts

Even the look of the text on the page says something about you and how you fit into a potential company. It's no mistake that Apple uses Myriad, The New York Times Magazine uses Garamond, or that the Obama campaign used Gotham – these fonts all have a specific feel and communicate to the viewer, regardless of what they spell out.

There are two very general font families: serif and sans serif. Serifed fonts are considered more serious, academic, highbrow. Sans serif fonts are great for future-facing industries like tech, trendy industries like marketing and PR, and they're generally considered less busy if you have to squeeze a lot of text into a small area.

Match the font to your talent set and where you're applying. If you're looking to do research at a law firm, serifs will make you appear smarter and more serious. A clean, sans serif font is probably the choice if you're going into design or social media.

And this should go without saying: fonts like Comic Sans, Papyrus, and Edwardian don't have any place on a resume. Go crazy on your birthday party invitations, but leave the fun fonts to your extracurriculars. No more than two different fonts on your resume; preferably just one. Chill on the all-caps versus small caps versus no caps stuff too. The rule? Make your materials easy on the eye so the reader can focus on the content.

Color

Since resumes are usually seen for the first time on a computer screen, adding a touch of color can be a good way to make your resume stand out. Keep a white background and black text, but augmenting the most important text with color, like your name or previous companies, can be a nice alternative to ALL CAPS. Color can count – green may be a strong choice if you're applying at Whole Foods or Starbucks, but don't use pink unless you're applying to do product development for Mattel.

Photo

In some industries, a thumbnail photo has become a standard resume element. Image-focused companies, like those in service and hospitality, often rely on attractive people to sell their product. In these cases, a photo can aid your search to prove you match the décor, so to speak.

The problem with a resume photo is that it flies in the face of Equal Employment Opportunity laws. As much as we'd like to think we live in a world where everyone is treated equally, we're not there yet, and studies still show that women and minorities are routinely discriminated against when applying for the same positions as white males. At the same time, some industries are more female-focused, and some companies may be specifically looking for minority candidates.

If you decide to add a photo to your resume, it absolutely must be professional quality. Don't show much skin. Smile approachably. Do not use your acting headshot because it will look like you're still an performer, just seeking another day job. Industry standards always apply.

Bonus Points

The savviest job-seekers have several different resumes ready to go. Feel free to tailor your skills and experience to different jobs or industries – the story you tell can capture different details depending on your goal.

Sending Your Resume

When emailing your resume, preserve your formatting by sending as a PDF attachment. If the company requests no attachments, have a version you can easily paste into email. I strongly caution against sending as an attachment in any format other than PDF – your recipient may not have the right computer or software to see the literature you've so very carefully curated.

Resume FAQ

Should I hire a professional resume writer?

Probably not. Use that money to buy drinks for someone in your target field while they give you tips on your current resume so you understand what is important in that industry and why. We're learning, not throwing money at the problem.

Do I have to update my resume for every job application?
No.

Can I use the same resume for jobs in different industries?
Probably not.

Why can't I include my college clubs and study abroad and GPA?

For the same reason you couldn't include your high school band camp on your performing resume. Plus, unless you were valedictorian and know the person reviewing your resume also loves Spain and thinks chess is cool, what you find impressive may just seem like distracting fluff. Save the dimension for your interview.

The Point

★ Your resume is the most important tool to outline why your experience is unique and useful.

★ Create your career narrative based on your actual experience.

★ Construct your resume to grab and hold the attention of your target audience.

Marketing

Creating Your Custom Career Campaign

Now you've got the resume – it's time to start sending it out as part of your total, fabulous package. But first, you'll want to be prepared with supporting materials to round out your narrative of why you're a strong candidate for your ideal position. Your career search is a marketing campaign – in order to sell yourself, it's time to be aggressive, intelligent, and strategic.

Because you are probably positioning yourself as a candidate for a job you've never had, in an industry you may have never worked, you have to go beyond just submitting your resume. You have to mitigate the risk for the person hiring by building a compelling case that you are the best one for the job.

This is where it becomes crucial to be a step ahead of the competition. The way you will do that is by thinking the way your future company thinks and becoming familiar with its goals and values, which will make your future boss's job easier before you even start.

Details count. I easily dismiss 90% of the applications I receive at my company due to lack of proper formatting, spelling, and grammar alone. In other words, while I am very open to entertaining varied work experience and career goals for junior-level applicants (versus a manager or director position, which usually requires very relevant experience), which isn't common in today's talent-rich market, I have to draw the line at anything less than an impeccable first impression.

I do love creativity in introductions – a personalized logo on a resume or clever turn of phrase in an intro letter -- but you don't get to branch out until you master the basics.

And here are the essentials, so listen up!

Your Marketing Materials

As a performer, career search marketing tools beyond your resume may have included your headshot, reel or intro video, audition repertoire, website, and beyond. Now you'll still be building a portfolio to showcase yourself, but instead of appearance or artistic talent, it will now be based on your experience, skills, and goals.

The necessary marketing materials for your new job search are your:

- Resume
- Intro Letter
- References
- Contact List
- Application Tracker

Here are explanations of these elements, after which we'll move onto the extras.

Intro Letter

Your introductory letter, also called a cover letter, tells more about you: your strengths, your story, and how they relate to the position at hand. It not only explains why you are a unique candidate, but also provides you with a platform to sell yourself by tailoring your pitch to explain how your skills and experience will benefit the company -- versus droning on about what you are seeking.

Your intro letter will take the form of an email when your resume is attached or pasted below. It is not optional. If you are considering not including the letter, it's a sign that you're favoring quantity of submissions over quality of jobs that truly interest you, and it will show.

Your letter must be personalized. Cut-and-paste doesn't cut it; it only takes five seconds to insert the company name and position into your letter, and that's the minimum that should be done to personalize your intro.

Your intro letter has to be excellently written. A company can't trust you to communicate on its behalf if you can't do so for yourself.

Just like the resume, think keywords over rapturous sentences. You can even bullet point your top qualities or experiences in your letter instead of a long paragraph. It's better to keep your cover letter brief and well-written. This is not a college essay; it's an opportunity to explain what is not in your resume, request a meeting, and prove you can communicate well.

Your cover letter is the opportunity to explain – and you must – any of these resume red flags:

- You've had too many jobs in too short a time period
- You've had lots of internships and no jobs
- You live in another city
- You're overqualified for the given position
- You are from another industry
- It looks like you're still pursuing another career

Tell your own story instead of letting someone else assume it for you.

If you're truly willing to move backward in your career status or income level, you must explain why. Is this the company of your dreams and you plan to stay for a long time? Do you want to acquire skills you may have skipped over in previous career development? Was your previous director role at a small company the equivalent of a manager role at this one? Don't try to gloss it over; proactively call it out so you can explain your motives.

The same goes for forging your way into a new industry. I'm a big champion of changing careers or industries if it's a deliberate decision, but if you're truly willing to move backward in your career/income level, you must explain why.

A recession-era complaint that I've heard more than once is that applicants have felt they were being turned down for jobs beneath their experience level. The answer to this conundrum – like most of the answers in this chapter – is found by putting yourself in the employer's shoes. The problem with over-qualification is that the company assumes it can't afford to pay you what you're worth, or it fears you won't be happy in this role and will leave the moment you find a more advanced position, meaning they will have to hire again in a few months. If you're truly excited about a role that seems to be a step backward, explain how you see it fitting into your career path.

Above all, this is the chance to tell your story, to build the narrative of who you are and why you are making this transition. It must read as a positive, optimistic, confident decision. Your employer is not your therapist; they're looking for someone they can plug into the position who's going to deliver.

References

In many cases, the word of your references is the final factor to tip things in your favor. Make sure these contacts are your biggest fans and ready to go to bat for you.

Most jobs ask for two or three references; it's wise to have more than that ready to go so you can tailor which references you supply depending on the job.

There are two types of references:

1. **Professional**: people who have worked with you in one of your past jobs, either as colleagues within your company or close contacts doing business with you.

2. **Personal**: people who know you outside of work.

In general, you don't have to supply references until they are requested. At that time, supply no more than four, complete with name, phone number, email address, their title and company where you worked together, or relationship if they are a personal reference.

Since your evaluator's time is valuable, make sure you are only supplying contacts who return phone calls and emails promptly.

A few rules for references:

1. **You must clear it with them first.** People elect to become your references, don't blindside one of your valuable contacts by forcing them to sing your praises without being able to think it through first.

2. **They must know you well.** This person can speak intelligently about how you handle situations from first-hand experience.

3. **They must be recent.** Your manager from ten years ago should not be asked to vouch for your work today.

4. **They must be credible.** It's better for a professional reference to be your superior rather than someone on your team, and for a personal reference to have a solid professional title, suggesting that they understand what makes a good employee.

5. **They cannot be family.** Even if you are Malia Obama, you cannot list a family member as a reference.

What to do with amazing references that know of you but can't necessarily speak at length about your work ethic? This is the time to secure a letter of reference that you can use as a supplemental application piece (see below). Supply the contact with specific notes about what the letter should say. As always, make your needs as easy to fulfill as possible for the person doing you this generous favor.

If you have a personal contact with a connection to your target company or potential boss, you absolutely can and should alert them that you are applying or even request a plug. Simply have them shoot an email to their contact at the company. Recently, a personal friend of mine was going in for an interview at a theatre production company and, in his research, saw that I was connected to the founder on Facebook (smart!). This now-producer had directed me in one of my first off-off Broadway plays way back in the day. So while I would not have been an appropriate formal reference for my friend, I was able to email my contact before his interview to establish the connection, giving him a leg up before he even walked in the door.

Nepotism is a real thing. Don't fight it; find a way to make it work for you.

Contact List

Your contacts are the single most important tool you have in your job search. Whether in one master list, or readily accessible through a combination of your phone, address book, and social media, you must have an accurate snapshot of who you know so you can figure out how they can support your search.

How you organize your contacts is up to you, but strengthening your current relationships while building your network will be invaluable, not just for your next job, but for your entire career. The next chapter, on networking, will delve into the how.

The Extras

Depending on the job, you may need supplemental materials to support your resume and letter, such as:

- Letters of reference
- Design portfolio
- Proof of certification
- Other work portfolio
- Writing samples
- Test results

Have these ready to go so that if one is requested, you can respond right away. Unlike most things in life, this *is* a competition, so position yourself to be in the lead at every step of the game.

Polish these pieces as carefully as you do your resume. As with your resume, they should be meticulously edited, designed well with minimal visual fuss, match the fonts and colors of your resume when possible, and be sent in PDF format.

You can also be creative about what makes you a great person to hire. My secret weapon was a one-sheet of brief but powerful testimonials from a variety of people who had worked with me, speaking less about a specific skill set and more about my work ethic and qualities that weren't dependent on the role at hand, like learning quickly and being personable with clients. It showed the value of my previous work, and a testimonial is almost always stronger than building one's own case. Find tangible ways to over-deliver in your application process.

Website

An online portfolio is a fantastic way to showcase your work. You likely had one as a performer, but a career search website can be far more simple (and with far fewer headshots). It also shows you know how to take initiative and build a showcase for yourself, suggesting you can also represent a company professionally and dynamically.

If you are still using your personal URL for your performance career, you have two choices: reorganize it so that it also supports where you are positioning yourself for your new career (i.e., separate pages for dancer, graphic designer, etc.), or create a second site that is job search specific.

Online Resumes

When you create a resume to be searchable on a job seekers' website, be sure to update it periodically so that it's always current. Keep a log of everywhere your resume lives online along with usernames, passwords, and direct link URLs. It's also helpful to have a cut-and-paste plain text version of your resume handy in a Word document for emails and form-based sites.

Video Resume

This is a trend that I don't typically recommend for non-performance careers unless it gives you an edge in the particular job or field to which you're applying. Let's hope it keeps shifting, but for now we're still in the age of discrimination issues, and allowing people to subconsciously judge you based on age, race, or other visual factors could work against you. Even if you have on-camera training, the way you come across visually is best saved for an interview where you can develop rapport with your interviewer.

If you do produce a video resume, it absolutely must be professionally shot and edited with state of the art lighting and sound. Again, no busy graphics, and keep it as brief as possible. Attention spans get shorter every day.

If you're searching for a job like spokesperson or even sales, a video resume could be a great investment to prove you're personable and present yourself well. But otherwise, spend the time and money building your professional contact network instead.

Social Media

Increasingly, nothing you do is private. Your posts, tweets, comments, and other online interactions are not only viewable by more people than you may think, but indexed for an Internet eternity. Of course, until now you've been meticulous about not posting drunken college party pictures or political rants online, so you're golden, right?

Some companies check social media profiles, even to the point of asking applicants to open their profiles while in an interview – probably a breach of privacy, but it's a competitive world out there – why risk it? On the other hand, if you're applying to a job where social media aptitude is a requirement, your active profiles may be fair game. Show intelligence and interest in your target field by who and what you follow, share, and post.

Even if your social media profiles aren't public, someone connected to a given company may have access to a photo or post that you don't want seen by a potential employer. It's good practice not to ever put anything online that you don't want everyone in the world to see.

Google yourself. Actively control your top results, which are usually Facebook, Twitter, YouTube, Vimeo, IMDb, and your personal site (www.yourname.com). Populate them with positive, accurate information about who you are and what you want people to know about you.

Your Process

A Note on Emailing Your Documents

Judging from my company's HR inbox, it bears repeating: *send your documents in PDF format*. A PDF ensures that it's just one click to view the document, and that any formatting you used will be preserved for the viewer.

Just as important: a document destined for someone else should be clearly labeled with your name and what it is (i.e., "Ciara Pressler – Resume"). That way, if someone saves it to a folder on their computer, it will be obvious what the document contains when it's listed alongside hundreds of others.

Be sure the subject line of your email references the position for which you're applying. If you have an inside contact or connection to the recipient or company, indicate this in the subject line or first sentence of your email. There must be text in the body of the email. And, as with your resume, make triple sure there are no grammar or spelling errors – instant grounds for deletion.

If I have tons of resumes to get through in a short period of time, I'll simply delete those that make me work too hard to read them. Make dealing with you – from application to interview – a breeze. Using common sense suggests you'll be easy to work with if hired.

(I am purposely not telling you how to create a PDF, because I want you to get in the habit of using resources like the Internet to learn how to do things yourself rather than to rely on someone else for tiny details. This section is more about the why than the how, and there is usually more than one way of doing tasks. Ultimately, taking initiative in things big and small will make you a professional force to be reckoned with.)

Finding Job Openings

A significant percentage of jobs go to people already connected to a given company, especially in arts and entertainment, making your contact list your most important tool. (Read on to the next chapter for networking and contact organization tips.)

In general, time spent building relationships and using your network for information and recommendations is going to be a smarter approach than applying to random job postings. One study showed that only 2% of jobs get filled through sites like Monster and Career Builder, so don't waste too much of your time submitting blindly. Think of these sites as research tools to know where the jobs are, and then use your connections and common sense to find another way in the door.

Jobs are posted in many more places than just the well-known sites. Searching on niche sites may also help you avoid being lost in a sea of competing applications. Especially if you are targeting a specific industry, find out where the companies that match your lifestyle lists are going to look for candidates. Professional organizations, industry-specific mailing lists, alumni associations, community organizations, and special interest groups are all fantastic resources for job listings.

Obviously, the internet changes daily. Let these sites be a jumping off point, but do your own searching to find out where there are more resources, especially for particular industries.

Tracking Your Applications

Measuring your process is vital. It's the only way to know whether you need to change something, or if you are making progress in a certain area.

As simple as a spreadsheet, this document tracks each and every job to which you've applied and what your results have been. You may have already been tracking auditions this way, in which case it's easy to just repurpose your current system for this one.

At minimum, you'll want to track the date, company, contact, and result information for each application sent. You can super-charge it with data on the industry, how you were referred/how you found out about the job, type of response, when you last followed up, etc.

Again, it doesn't matter how you organize your information internally, it matters that you do track it, and that you have a system that works for you. Don't make it so vague that you can't easily analyze your progress, but don't make it so complicated that you're spending more time tracking than executing.

Quantity and quality should both help you perfect your process. Make it a numbers game. If you have applied for 40 jobs and been called in for two interviews, you can estimate that you have to apply for about 20 more before you get the next in-person meeting. No big deal. Just do the math and let it direct your work.

Also note which types of companies and industries tend to respond to you. If you like them, refocus your effort to that specific area. If you don't, change up your materials to better target the companies you do want.

Extra Credit Tips

Always, always be honest. Don't try to guess what they're looking for; be honest, clear, and descriptive so they can make an informed decision.

Some of the best applications I've seen very honestly explain traditional "no-no's" – gaps in employment, lots of turnover, transition from another career or industry. Control your own image by narrating your own story.

If you really want the job, search someone from the company on Facebook or LinkedIn and find out if you have a contact in common who can put in a good word for you.

Bottom line: it's a competitive market in any field. As with all things in business, make others' lives and jobs easier, and you will be more successful.

Staying Motivated

Treat your career search like a job of its own: create consistency by setting mini-goals or defined hours when you'll focus on your search. Whether it's being at the same coffee shop for two hours each day, or sending out your resume at least 10 times each week, having smaller milestones will help you feel like you are making progress.

Own up to when you need a shot of inspiration – pepper in some informational interviews, read another career book, or grab a friend to meet with once a week as an accountability partner, setting goals for the week ahead and checking in as you go. And be sure to keep restorative activities on your calendar, whether it's a yoga class or a movie night. Keep yourself focused, but make it fun!

The Point

★ Your intro letter is the most powerful opportunity to tell your career transition story.

★ Use additional materials to give yourself an edge over the competition.

★ Track your actions to assess your progress and improve your process.

Networking

Mastering the Art of Flattery

Remember your favorite concert performance, your best choreography collaboration, your memorable film that played the festival circuit? And someone – you didn't even know! – went out of their way to compliment your work. It could have been high school; it could have been last month. It's time to take all those compliments and use them as fuel to start projecting the same appreciation back out into the world.

There are amazing people doing amazing things in every single industry, every city, every job out there. And now it's time to meet them, find out what makes them tick, and leave a positive impression so that when they hear of a job opening, the first person they think of is you.

It's Not About You

Mention the word "networking," and you'll get roughly the same reaction to "root canal." So many people hate the idea of networking or, more accurately, their misperception on what networking is and how it's done that they've become intimidated to the point of opting out altogether.

Being intimidated by networking is simply not a valid excuse. There is nothing to be afraid of when it comes to meeting new people, especially if you've stood on stage in front of hundreds of people and bared your soul. Networking becomes loathsome when you equate it to shameless self-promotion, which it is not nor should it be.

What is networking? Connecting with people. You are a pro at this. You do this daily. From your barista to your mail carrier to accepting a new friend request, you come into contact with someone unfamiliar every single day. Beyond that, you constantly reconnect with those you already know – catching up, sharing information, even helping one another. And, chances are, you do this without dissolving into a fit of embarrassment or pomposity.

The trick to embracing networking is this: It's Not About You. Simply focus on what the other person has to say, and truly listen – what are their needs? What are they trying to accomplish? What makes them excited? The wisest thing I ever heard said about human interaction is that people will forget what you say, but they will never forget how you made them feel. And everyone wants to be heard.

An American queen of person-to-person selling, Mary Kay Ash, coached her budding salespeople to pretend everyone is wearing a sign that says "Make me feel important." Be on their team from the start. Sending the energy of positive support will take you further than the most perfectly crafted elevator pitch any day.

How to Network Effectively

Networking is a means to an end. The end is creating a useful and dynamic contact database. Here are the means:

1. Get them talking.

Flip our It's Not About You premise to the positive and remember: It's About Them. Your primary goal is to find out about the individual you're meeting so you can follow up in a sincere, concrete way. And pay attention! There's nothing worse than walking away from a conversation and forgetting what was said – plus, the person talking will inevitably sense it if your mind is elsewhere.

So how do you get someone talking? Ask questions. Not random questions out of the blue – start with something based on why you're face-to-face in the first place: "How do you know the host?" or "Are you a member of this organization?" Then the following questions are based on what they've told you – which not only makes you listen carefully to cues for what your next question might be but it also signals that you're truly listening.

2. Get their contact information.

Rather than shoving your business card into a hand otherwise occupied with hors d'oeuvres, the best way to end an interaction is to ask for the new contact's information. This puts the ball in your court to follow up – you're not left hoping that they will contact you. Grab a pen and make a note of where you met them or other identifying details so you can jog your memory when following up.

3. Make your impression based on your audience.

While having a rehearsed 10-second pitch can be useful for narrowing down your purpose and what you want people to remember about you, what's most memorable is how you can help the person in front of you. Try to find a connection: what you have in common and why you might want to stay in contact past this initial meeting.

And if you have nothing else in common, it helps to have a fall-back fun fact. I usually create an impression when mentioning that I'm training for a road race – even if someone's not a runner, they know one or have a strong enough opinion on the absurdity of distance running that it adds dimension. Either way, it makes a dent in their immediate consciousness, and who knows – next time they glimpse a runner, it might jog (ha) their memory of meeting me.

4. Follow up.

First impressions are important, but continuing contact is the key to growing your personal network. Don't wait too long to remind your new contact that you met and what you're all about. Keep it brief, friendly, and appropriate to the person's status and how you met.

Flattery vs. Appreciation

A note on making it All About Them: It's painfully transparent when a compliment is given or attention is paid purely for the sake of flattery. As much as I love compliments, I forget them instantly when they're insincere because I start focusing on figuring out what this person wants from me and whether I plan to give it to them.

A compliment paid is infinitely better than a compliment thought. But if it's just not the time or place, wait for a better opportunity. There are few better follow-ups than to tell a new contact that you were inspired by her entrepreneurism or that his hosting skills rival Martha Stewart. Just keep it sincere, authentic, and balanced, and your respect will be well-received.

Identifying Your Network

Great news! You already have a robust network. And it's big. Every person you've ever met is a candidate, from schoolmates to colleagues to fellow artists.

Especially as an artist, you encounter more people than the average professional since your projects probably change with more frequency, bringing so many accessible opportunities to meet more people. Ideally you've kept all those contact sheets, saved those cc'd emails, and can gather all the people you've met into one central place. Even if someone you know doesn't have the information you need, they are connected to hundreds of other people who might.

Now it's time to go through your mental and physical contact database and consolidate it so you can maximize your communications. Professionally, add every job reference, every current and former colleague at your day job, and every current and former collaborator in any artistic endeavor.

That includes:

Day Job:
- Boss
- Coworkers
- Clients
- Contacts
- Vendors

Artistic Career:
- Performers
- Directors
- Producers
- Agents/managers
- Casting directors
- Creatives
- Photographers
- Coaches
- Teachers
- Board members
- Organization admins
- Organization members
- Volunteers

You can also draw from your personal circle when appropriate. Who in your personal life is plugged into interesting professional networks?

Personal Life:
- Family
- Friends
- Neighbors
- Former professors
- Personal vendors – trainer, dog walker, bartender, etc.
- Family of friends
- Social network connections

Organizing Your Contacts

It's going to be difficult to maintain your contacts if you can't figure out who's who. Create a simple system that's effective for you. When you need to get in touch with that woman you met that time at that place, it should only take a moment to track down her email address.

I can be horrible with names and even faces, but I like to say I never forget a skill set. So I organize business cards by industry as it pertains to what I do – media, artists, event vendors, party attendees, publicists, clients, venues, etc. My own simple system is mostly spreadsheets with separate columns for role, company, industry, and keywords. This way, if I need a magazine contact, I can just run a simple search. Or if I want to invite all of my film contacts to a screening, it's easy to sort and send.

The sophistication of your contact management system is entirely up to you, from Outlook to iCloud to FileMaker, but always remember that contact organization is a means to an end. Don't get so caught up in making it perfect that you procrastinate the whole point of maintaining your contacts which is to *contact them*.

After recording your contacts and backing up that record (no "I lost my phone!" excuses are acceptable in the 21st century, people), the most important thing you can do is prioritize your contacts. Create a hierarchy, because some people will need to be kept up to date more than others.

Supporting Cast

These are the people who will go to bat for you any day of the week. They forward you job postings, talk to their contacts on your behalf, get excited when you meet a major milestone. Even if it's just a handful of people, your inner circle is the most valuable part of your network.

Directors

These are your references and mentors; those whose endorsements or affiliations validate what you're doing. These are the people to ask (always ask first!) to list as references in job applications, testimonials for your website, or endorsements on LinkedIn. Keep them happy. Write thank-you notes any time they endorse or otherwise go out of their way for you.

Audience
This is your entire existing network. These people get the major updates, including when you get a new job or leave an old one, invites to events you're hosting, or major milestones like press, a degree, or another accomplishment.

In the Wings
These are the people you want to move up the totem pole, but either you don't know them well enough yet or you have yet to meet them at all. This is your contact hit list, and it may take building some more one-on-one rapport before sending the constant news stream the rest of your network receives.

Growing Your Network

While it's important to continually grow and maintain your professional network, quality should always take priority over quantity. Yes, it's lovely to have 1,000 Facebook friends if you're having a garage sale, but, if you haven't seen half of them in real life in the past few years, what stake will they have in helping you find work?

Networking happens both online and off. Nearly every industry has professional organizations that hold events, from happy hours to conferences. Many of these are free to attend, but those with a fee are often well worth it – not only are you meeting a significant number of people in your chosen field, but you're also gaining industry expertise and credibility by associating yourself with a wider organization. Sign up for newsletters from your target industry's umbrella organizations to find out about upcoming events. If you're new to the game, volunteer to work on an event. You'll get to know the organizers and you stand a better chance of interacting with the more established participants.

Staying in Touch

I'm a news addict, so whenever I see an article that pertains to something one of my contacts is doing, I send it with a quick note. This shows I'm thinking about them and frames me as someone who is supportive and attentive to their goals. Who wouldn't want someone like that on his or her team?

The best periodic updates I get are from Kyle, a professional contact I've known for seven years, having collaborated on several occasions. A playwright and composer who's constantly juggling new projects from scripts to bands to performances, his updates are short and sweet and humble, and include all the pertinent information.

Subject: Super Mirage Friday / Hypochondria Launch

Happy Monday! I wanted to let you know about a couple things I have coming up:

1. ***Super Mirage, this Friday at Pianos.*** *My band Super Mirage will be cranking out our patented brand of highly danceable jams this Friday 3/4 at 11pm at Pianos (158 Ludlow Street). Admission just $10. More info here.*

2. ***Launch party for Hypochondria.*** *On Sunday March 13th from 7-10pm, at Under St. Mark's Theatre (94 St Mark's). Just $10 with proceeds to benefit an upcoming production of my play Hypochondria in April, directed by Jimmy Maize as part of the Columbia Graduate Directing Program. At the launch party there'll be performances from special guests Libby Winters, Clay McLeod Chapman, and my new music collaboration with Lauren Worsham. More info here.*

All the best,
Kyle
www.landoftrust.com

Done. I have all the info I need, and, if I want to know more, there are links. No fluff, just facts. He could go on and on about the ten other projects he has in the works and what these projects mean to him and *isn't it cold outside today you guys?*, but he consistently sticks to the latest, and always in the same format, and as a result, I always open and read Kyle's emails because I know what I'm in for and that I can easily digest it. If a project is particularly important to him, he sends me a personal follow-up email.

Best of all, when I email Kyle, he always writes back within minutes with a *Thank You*, or my favorite: *You Rock!* It leaves a warm fuzzy feeling that makes me want to support anything he does, and even though we first collaborated many years ago, I still send contacts his way whenever I come across someone who could benefit his career.

When It's Appropriate to Ask

The best and most appropriate time to send a mass message to your entire audience is when:

1. **You change jobs.** Include your new company, title, and contact information, as well as the types of things you'll be working on – you'll get your contacts thinking early about how you can collaborate.

2. **You have news that could lead to more work.** Perhaps you landed a major account, were featured in a magazine, won an award, or some other accomplishment that relates to what your network needs.

Always keep your news blasts extremely brief and to the point. If you're worried about sounding braggy, simply deliver the facts only, and perhaps add a special thank you to whomever helped you land that success to show that you don't forget acts of kindness. Generosity is contagious and usually comes back to you in unexpected ways.

When Not to Network

When working as the marketing director for a film festival several years ago, I had to pull aside an actress who was using her volunteer access as a way to slip her headshot to directors and producers attending the festival. I explained to her that this was not the appropriate time for aggressive self-promotion – the filmmakers were there to be honored and to celebrate their enormous accomplishment, not to cast their next project. Rather than creating a positive impression, she was positioning herself as someone to avoid because she didn't know how to behave appropriately in a high-stakes situation.

Personal events are almost always a bad time to network. Weddings, funerals, baby showers, receptions, birthdays – yes, you'll meet new people, but don't make a professional pitch beyond mentioning what you do if asked. Feel free to give those you meet information about you, but hold off on selling yourself unless the opportunity tactfully presents itself.

This is a great time to use what I call the Two-Time Technique: rather than hit someone up the first time you meet them, use the second encounter to broach the topic of business. If you meet a hiring manager at a birthday dinner, don't start grilling her about interview techniques during her leisure time. Instead, email her a few days later and keep it friendly:

> *Hi Adrienne –*
>
> *It was great to meet you at Aparna's bridal shower! I'm not sure anyone ever uses a lemon zester either, but I'm sure it will be the key to a long & happy marriage.*
>
> *You mentioned that you work at JetBlue – I've been researching jobs in travel, so if you have any advice it would be much appreciated!*
>
> *Looking forward to seeing you at the wedding – I can already tell the reception will be a dance party for the record books.*
>
> *Cheers,*
> *Pamela*

By moving the "ask" to the second time you come in contact, you avoid looking opportunistic by plugging yourself at someone else's celebration.

When it comes to online networking no's, just remember that all of us are inundated daily with emails, posts, and tweets. Pick your intrusions wisely so you'll be noticed when it's truly important. Balance queries about work with reminders that you are a desirable hire – link to a relevant article on Facebook or Twitter, email information about an industry event, or post an inspirational quote from a leader in your field.

And it's an incredibly wonderful thing to raise money for a charitable project, but it puts your professional contacts in an awkward position to hit them up for donations, especially if you incorporate a TMI personal story. Be very picky when asking people for very personal support.

When in doubt, keep in mind my number-one communication rule – It's About Them, not you – and the appropriate time, place, and way to network will become increasingly clear.

The Point

★ It's Not About You: make every interaction a chance to make an authentic connection.

★ Organize your contacts in a way that lets you find people quickly and easily.

★ Communicate appropriately – the right people, the right timing, and the right messaging.

Interview

The Non-Performance Audition

Congratulations, you have an interview! Unlike most auditions, far fewer candidates are called in to meet in person. An interview invitation signals a serious interest in you as a candidate. So this is a big deal!

It's your time to shine: after years of auditioning, you are an interview machine. Whereas an average job applicant goes years without interviewing, as a performer, you're auditioning often, so your skills are polished. All you have to do now is channel your ability to show up and deliver into the dynamics of a conventional interview.

Since you're not walking in with a book of 16-bar song options, preparation is in order. It's time to get your inner game, as well as your outer game, ready to make a lasting impression.

The point of an interview is not just to show your talent; it's to tell your story and build rapport with the interviewer, as well as to find out if this is the right company and position for you. Think less performance or therapy session and more first date or meeting the parents – be at your best and make it a dialogue.

Before the Interview

The second you schedule the interview, it's time to shift into reconnaissance mode. You're now a high-level detective, finding out everything you can about the company, its leadership, and, if possible, the person with whom you will interview.

Here's what to review, in this order:

1. **The Company Website.** Read as much of it as possible, not only to find out more about the company, but also to understand how it talks about itself and what it aspires to be. The website is usually a company's best possible representation of itself, so understand how it wants to be portrayed and how you fit into that image.

2. **Social Media.** These are third-party sites where the company manages its own presence, like Facebook, Twitter, LinkedIn, and YouTube. What is the company saying, does it have fans and followers, and how does it interact with the public?

3. **Media Coverage.** A simple search can deliver press coverage, legal issues, and even financials. Is the company healthy and stable? In an aggressive growth period? Showing signs of panic? Like an investor, start to research whether the company is a solid bet for your time and talent.

4. **What other people say about the company.** Check user reviews and comments on sites like Yelp, FourSquare, and Angie's List. A simple Google search will deliver press, user reviews, and other coverage. While individual user reviews and comments can be weak evidence, you can look for trends, red flags, and, most importantly, see how a company responds (or doesn't) in a crisis. Check Glassdoor and LinkedIn for clues on how past employees felt about the company.

5. **The Leadership.** Who's in charge and what is their background? Do they have a track record of success? Have they written books or articles you can scan for information on their general business philosophies?

6. **The Interviewer.** If you're not interviewing with the boss, see if you can find out some basic info on the interviewer. Don't be creepy, but if their bio is on the company website, it's fair game, as is anything on their LinkedIn profile. Use social media to see if you have any contacts in common.

7. **The Job Description.** Read carefully through the requirements and duties so you are prepared to talk about the specific experience that prepares you for the role at hand.

Not all of the information you uncover will be appropriate to bring up in the interview, but it will certainly inform your conversation. It will show if you have done your research, understanding the company's mission and how your unique talents and skills support it. On the flipside, you'll know if you're being given the runaround about company growth and culture if it isn't supported by third-party reports.

Your cover letter may have already explained your story, but the interview is your chance to tell it and to note what interviewers respond to so you can continue to hone the narrative. While it's impossible to know exactly what will come up in an interview, there are several questions common enough to have answers prepped in advance:

- Tell me about yourself…
- What made you interested in this position?
- Why are you interested in this company?
- Where do you see yourself in five years?
- Any questions for me?

There are endless articles easily found online covering both common interview questions and suggestions for strong answers – definitely review two or three and think about how you'll answer the most universal questions. But above all, be prepared with a few thoughtful questions about the company and the position. It's not just about how well you answer questions, but also about what you want to find out.

And remember: in the "real world," certain evaluation factors are off limits by law. As if you weren't already grateful enough not to list your weight and height on your resume, discrimination on the basis of age, sex, religion, disability, and, in many cases, sexual orientation, is illegal, so be cautious about speaking in a way that suggests a special consideration based on any of the above.

The things that should go without saying but must be said: put the interview in your mobile calendar along with all the details – when, where, who, direct contact information. Map it in advance and add extra travel time just in case. Confirm your interview the day before not only to make sure it's still on their calendar, but also to suggest to the company that you're super-organized and excited to meet them.

Which of course brings us to the most important topic...

What to Wear

The rule of thumb is this: dress appropriately for the job or industry while maintaining your personal style. Every industry has a style – conservative or trendy; formal or casual. But even if you are going in for a job where the dress code is laid-back, dress business-casual at minimum. A three-piece suit will read as out-of-touch, but slacks and a nice shirt are appropriate without alienating.

Ladies: go easy on trends and keep the legs and cleavage tucked in. Men: tailoring is everything. Yes, there are exceptions... if you are interviewing to be the manager of a strip club or for pretty much any role at American Apparel. Even if you're interviewing in the fashion industry, going classic with a modern flair instead of over-the-top trendy shows good judgment.

If you're truly clueless about what to wear, go to an area of your town where people from your target industry hang out and watch them go by before work, during lunch, or after work. You'll see themes you can imitate.

If you have a particular personal style, you can incorporate it within reason. I love vintage, but head-to-toe Mad Men style would be far too costume-y for a first meeting, so I maintain my style in business settings with a classic suit and a piece of my grandmother's jewelry. By all means, rock your signature color or that piece you feel incredible wearing, but never use the interview as an opportunity to find out if you can walk in five-inch heels or to squeeze into the pants from ten pounds ago.

Take the what-to-wear stress out of your interview prep by predetermining your go-to interview outfits in advance, down to the accessories. Instead of sartorial stress, use the pre-interview period to study up on your future employer.

At the Interview

It all starts with your arrival, which is where the rules of auditioning are nearly identical. Be at least 15 minutes early so that you can survey the scene and get into your zone before going into the room. If you're going to a large building with check-in procedures and travel time between the front desk and your destination, account for this. Same goes for finding parking, dealing with mass transit, or that last-minute shot of espresso.

Like an audition moderator, the receptionist or HR rep is not someone to gloss over. For all you know, he or she has a say in the hiring and may be discussing candidates with the decision maker. This could be your future coworker, so make a great first impression by being both professional and kind. The hiring process is complicated and stressful for those conducting the interviews as well as for interviewees, so be conscientious of their time and attention.

Unlike an audition, which is a mini-performance, an interview is a dialogue. It's not just about your talent; it's about what the interviewer has to say about the company and the position. The most important thing you can do to become an excellent interviewer is to share the spotlight. Just as in networking, make the interviewer feel important my letting him or her speak. Find out not just about the job itself, but the company culture and long-term trajectory.

Magic started happening when I shifted the energy of my interviews from the "God I hope I get it" mentality of an auditioner to the "Here's what I have to offer" approach of a star. But when I upped it to "How can I help you meet your goals?" things really started taking off. Marc Cenedella, CEO of TheLadders.com, reports that the single most effective interview question is when a candidate asks her potential boss, "How can I help you get a gold star on your review next year?" This shows concern for the needs of the company and priorities of the management – exactly the person I want on my team. While that exact question may not be appropriate, pre-formulating questions like this will make you stand out as someone who's willing to meet the demands of the job and fit into the company culture.

When you're interviewing with the human resources representative, take the opportunity to find out more about the company and its culture, not just the specific job and benefits. If you come away interested in the company itself, you can follow up about other positions even if the initial job isn't the right fit. The human resources contact becomes a new and very valuable person on your list.

After the Interview

The very first thing you must do after the interview is to send a thank you note. A thank-you is a courteous gesture and good business etiquette. When I'm deciding between two candidates, the thank you note is what sways me. Even if I don't hire the candidate, if she cares enough to express gratitude for my time, I'll remember her if she's right for a future role.

I'm a huge fan of a classic written note, but time is of the essence, so email is perfectly acceptable. You want to stay fresh in their minds and appear more prompt than other candidates. Send a note to every person you met, if possible. Keep your message short, sincere, and confident. Reiterate your interest in the role as well as why you are a strong candidate.

For extra credit, drop in a reference to something you discussed in the interview, especially a personal item like shared love of tennis or this weekend's jazz festival. It shows that you listen, can provide useful information, and that you'll be someone they want to be around every day.

This is a good thank you note:

Dear Ms. Boggio,

Thank you for meeting with me today! I truly enjoyed learning about Pressler Collaborative and your goals for the company. In light of my experience with high-profile events and your fall calendar of client events, I know I would be a strong addition to your team.

Below is the contact information for three references, as requested. I've sent each of them an email letting them know you may be contacting them.

Here is the book I mentioned from my marketing seminar: [Amazon link]. I hope you enjoy it!

Sincerely,
Avery Leader
503-555-3482
Avery.Leader@email.com

The message can be shorter. It should not be much longer. It can and should be more formal if you're applying in an industry that uses a very formal communication style, like law or education.

If, after the interview, you know that this is not the job for you, you should still send a thank you note. You never know if another, more appropriate job will open up at the same company or a company that is connected to the interviewer – or if the interviewer will end up being the hiring manager at your dream job three years from now. Always build your network!

Second Interviews

For most jobs, there is someone else you have to meet before you get an offer. The first interviewer screens out candidates; the most promising ones make it through the gatekeeper to the decision makers.

This is your chance to get more specific and ask questions that may have surfaced based on your initial interview. Do any additional research you can beforehand, and again, be prepared with thoughtful questions. The nature of questions in a second interview will go deeper into your experience and approach, and you may have to "sell" yourself more aggressively now that the competition has narrowed. I can remember the specific moment in each of my marketing career interviews where my answer to a second-interview question visibly convinced my future boss that I was the one to hire.

The second interview is also a chance for your future team, boss, or the executives to size up whether you're the right type for the company. Rather than let that intimidate you, make sure the company is a right fit for *you*. Ask about how they approach projects, interact with one another, measure success. I want you to worry less about hours, compensation, and benefits at this stage, and instead, focus more on whether this job is aligned with your career vision, lifestyle, strengths, and skills.

Great news: unlike callbacks, you don't have to wear the same outfit. In fact, please don't. The same style rules apply, except this time you have an inside view of how to visually position yourself as a potential part of the team.

Group Interviews

As a performer, you understand the importance of seeing how you meld with the team. As a second or third interview, you may be asked to spend time with a department or even with multiple applicants so they can see all of you simultaneously. Again, make sure you're conscious of give-and-take, but be sure to stick your neck out whenever it's appropriate.

The opportunity to interact with your future team can be the most crucial step in your interview process. It's like auditioning to become a replacement in a touring show that's been on the road for years – it isn't just about you being the best talent for the role. There is an established energy, rapport, and general way of doing things that you must adopt. At the end of the day, we want to work with the best people to be around for eight-plus hours each day, so again, be professional but warm and open to being part of the team.

Special Requests

On occasion, you'll be asked to jump additional hurdles before getting a job offer. Salespeople may be asked to formulate a pitch for a potential client; copywriters could be asked to take a grammar exam. The company is asking for additional evidence so it can be confident you're the best possible candidate.

I personally find it unethical to ask people not yet on a company's team to do formal work, but sometimes it's either necessary to see how someone will approach a project, and you may want this job enough that you are willing to show what you can do. If you feel uneasy about the request, you can ask for clarification or give an answer that shows your general approach but is too vague to be actionable by someone else. You can also supply examples of past work that is similar and shows you would be able to handle the task in a professional capacity.

The Point

★ Your audition skills are the perfect prep for acing any interview.

★ Research the company and its goals to get an edge over your competition.

★ Approach the interview as a problem-solver: you are the solution.

Acceptance

Evaluating Options and Negotiating Terms

And then, you get an offer.
You either want the job, don't want the job, or you aren't sure.
Here's what to do.

You Don't Want the Job

If you know this isn't the job for you, write a very polite and grateful email declining the offer. At the risk of being repetitive, you never know if you'll work with this company or the people involved in the future, so keep all bridges intact. You don't have to be specific about your reason for declining – keep it simple and professional.

> *Dear Mr. Benjamin,*
>
> *Thank you for your offer for the position of project manager at Kentbeck Golf. Unfortunately, I am declining at this time.*
>
> *Again, thank you for your time, and I wish you success in your future endeavors.*
>
> *Sincerely,*
> *August Zander*

You Want the Job

Nine times out of ten, this means it's time to negotiate.

This is when it's crucial to shed any of the "thank god I just got a job!" mentality that can be common with performers. One of the biggest obstacles you will struggle with coming out of the competitive, oversaturated performing arts is correctly valuing your skills.

The acceptance of nearly any job involves a dance of back-and-forth; it's about handling it well and getting what you need to start on a strong note. In any negotiation, you are teaching the other party what you are worth and where you will compromise.

Start by understanding the typical compensation for your position, factoring in your city and company size, by using a site like Salary.com. If you have any inside information from a friend in the industry or at the company, this is even more important. The bottom line is this: once you start at a particular level of compensation, it's unlikely you'll get a raise in the double percentage points, so start as high as you reasonably can.

With big companies, procedures like benefits and raises are typically instituted, but especially with small companies, everything is up for negotiation. Your compensation package is not just salary (and commissions, if applicable), but benefits like health insurance, 401K contributions, and both paid and unpaid days off including holidays, vacation, personal, and sick days. Your working conditions may also be relevant, including hours, travel, expense reimbursements, and to whom you report.

You must have all the specifics in writing. Don't be paranoid, but don't be naïve either: if their explanation for a lower starting salary is that you'll have a raise in six months, sort it out now. No need to be overly pushy; a simple, "Great! Can you add that in the letter of agreement?" will do.

As always, be prompt and professional with your negotiations and paperwork. Do everything you can to start this new relationship off on the right foot.

You Aren't Sure

That's okay – this is a big decision! Let's start by narrowing it down to *what* you aren't sure about.

> **Compensation.** Was the offer lower than you expected? Are they being unclear about benefits or schedule? See above – often, these things can be worked out.

> **The Position.** If you're sure you don't want this particular job but you like the company, talk to them about the possibility of tailoring the role so that everyone's needs are met. If the company is growing, is there a possibility of getting acclimated through this position and then moving forward into a different one? Often it's best just to get your foot in the door so you can navigate the company from the inside.

> **The Company.** If something about the company or its culture doesn't sit right, pay attention. Do the people there seem unhappy? Is there high turnover? Are they in crisis mode or, perhaps worse, stagnant? Once a company goes bad, it's hard to turn it around. You'd probably do well to keep looking amongst their competitors.

> **Your Boss.** Sharp inhale. There is turnover at companies all the time, meaning your boss isn't necessarily a permanent fixture, but having a terrible boss can severely alter your well-being both in and out of the office. Carefully weigh the pros and cons of interacting with this person daily – can you balance it with other work and other people, or is it going to be an uphill battle? Generally, if you're part of a team, managing a difficult personality is just a good skill to learn in order to grow as a professional and as a person.

> **Fear of Change.** There will probably be some lingering apprehension about your new career path, and that's to be expected. This is a major life change, and you're navigating

uncharted territory. But often, the best things in life happen by taking a leap. So many of my best experiences were initially timid decisions, but soon after taking the plunge, I felt incredibly fortunate and perfectly placed.

If there's just a nagging instinct that this isn't the right fit, honor that. You've done a lot of work and research not just about the job, but about yourself and what you want. Be confident that something else is around the bend.

Managing Expectations

When starting out on a new career path, you may not feel like you're in a position to ask for anything more than what a company initially offers. But you can build confidence by arming yourself with information about appropriate compensation for the role, company, and city where the job exists. Any smart company is going to try to get the best talent for the lowest price; it's your job to get as much as you can without being ridiculous.

As performers, we are conditioned to value work for the sake of work. This results in a gross undervaluing of what we do and no "fair market value" assessment of performance as a skilled profession. It's important to recognize this and begin to shake the willingness to be undercompensated.

Still, it is usually worth it to get your foot in the door in order to gain experience and contacts. My first post-performer job started as a part-time role, meaning no benefits and not enough income to cover my living expenses. But something inside me was so lit up by the company and what I could do there that I jumped in. Within two months, the job had increased to full-time. Soon after, I negotiated a higher salary. I gave myself time to get adjusted and gave the company time to see my value so that I had leverage. They also allowed and even encouraged me to take freelance projects on the side, which ultimately built the foundation for the company I started just four years later.

Getting Started

Between taking on a whole new job and adjusting to a new lifestyle, there's enough to be nervous about, so do everything you can to make it fun! Scope out new places to grab lunch. Shop for a few fresh pieces for your work wardrobe. Celebrate over drinks with friends or a special dinner with family.

At your new job, while your initial focus will undoubtedly be on learning the ropes, make building relationships a top priority. On the best days and worst days, it will be the people around you that make everything worth it. And as you move forward, these contacts will shape the next steps in your professional – and even personal – path.

Above all, look back to your reward from your self-designed Career Vision and DO IT! You have earned it, my amazing and gainfully employed friend.

The Point

★ Use your Career Vision, research, and gut instinct to evaluate job offers.

★ Start off on the best foot possible with your compensation package.

★ Celebrate your success!

Encore

Welcome to the Elite Society of Former Performers

Once you're solidly in your new chapter, you join the ranks of the Former Performers: the passionate souls who pursued one of the most difficult – and rewarding – career paths that exist. You followed your first dream, and that is something you should always cherish.

For a long time, I struggled with the admission that I used to be an actor. I thought it undermined my current career or suggested that I had failed and cashed out. As time gives me distance, however, I realize that my time as a performer contributed incredible value to both my new career path and the way I approach life. We all have our own journeys, and it is always better to have gone after your dream at the time it was right for you.

Instead of a liability, my years as an actor have come in incredibly useful for my post-performer jobs. I've carved out a marketing niche with companies that target artists; I'm quick on my feet in interviews with my improvisational training; I've stepped in to emcee client events at a moment's notice with (almost) no stage fright. Some lucky opportunities are personal – I once spent eight days in Costa Rica because a handsome guy recognized me from my last film role... now that's what I call residuals.

You should – you must – keep dreaming. Be open to evolving, and to acknowledging how you've grown or changed. In the words of Sondheim, "facing facts, not escaping them / still with dreams, just reshaping them."

Staying Involved in the Arts

If everything goes as planned, I'll spend my retirement directing campy musical revivals at a tiny community playhouse in some beach town. Until then, there are infinite ways to keep creativity a central part of life.

Heather, now a lawyer in Chicago, started her career as a dancer with a degree from NYU's Tisch School of the Arts. Her second degree in political science proved useful when she took a break from performing to intern in D.C., eventually going to law school, but she found herself missing dance immensely. While her new career in entertainment law allows her to work with artists on licensing and creative rights, she has made time in her schedule to perform in community dance events and pursue her Pilates teaching certification.

There is value in performing for performing's sake. You don't have to practice singing in order to audition for a role, you can sing because you just love it. You'll find that feeding your creative soul not only makes you better in business but also more balanced in life.

Staying Creative

There's no reason to limit yourself to what you practiced professionally. Now that you have creative development energy to spare, why not try another creative outlet? Visual arts, writing, crafts, cooking: there are a lot of creative endeavors outside of performing, and it's incredibly freeing to learn and develop art without the measurement of how far you're coming along professionally. If you don't love it, drop it and try something else. There is nothing to lose.

Giving Back

As your time and financial stability grows, you may find yourself in the incredibly lucky position to patronize the arts. What a wonderful way to give back to the field that helped you grow into the diverse professional you are today!

You don't have to be independently wealthy to support the arts. As you well know, time and talent are also valuable. As are connections – the people you meet in your new career may be the perfect contacts for a company that's near and dear to your heart.

One of the first moments I knew I could be happy as a former performer was in the audience of the first viBe Theater Experience show in 2002. chandra, my friend and theatrical collaborator, had started a program for inner-city teenage girls to create their own work and express themselves on stage. I anticipated a cringe-worthy show (hello, high school) and was totally floored by one of the most moving pieces of theatre I have ever seen, period. And I was struck with the thought that I would rather fund this work than be part of it. Ten years later, I got to serve on the host committee for their annual benefit, leveraging my contacts for silent auction donations and my press list for added exposure.

Carving Your Career Path

As an artist at heart, you will thrive by continuing to grow and create, both personally and professionally. Developing your career is a creative endeavor – no two paths are identical, and shaping yours will be a lifelong pursuit. You may take time off to travel or start a family. You may decide it's time to change careers again. All of this is fine, fantastic even, and I hope you now have a framework you can use again to focus on a new goal.

Never stop exploring. Keep learning – developing professionally and personally. Don't let a job or your age or your stage in life ever be an excuse to get stagnant.

Your life, your happiness, and your well-being, are utterly and completely worth it.

ExitStageRight.org

Join the community of former performers online for additional resources and recommendations, including books, classes, programs, and people who can help you with your transition. Get connected for news, event invitations, and fresh advice to navigate your transition successfully.

Thanks

Betsy and Jodie Capes, for seeing my performing experience as an asset when you hired me for my first post-transition job. Our two years together were best marketing and business boot camp possible.

Allison Mullen, for day job support that gave me human resources (and happy hour) experience.

The New York office of Congresswoman Carolyn B. Maloney, for the internship that got me through my transition. And for not offering me a political job before I took the marketing one.

Carol Keane and Christina Faraj, for the freelance gig that got me through my transition.

Alicia Rebensdorf and Brandon Kienzle, for inspiring the discipline to write something longer than an article.

Alicia, Maite Alvarez, Nzingtha Smith, Megan Meiklejohn, Michael Hammerstrom, Akari Yanada, and Cordarro Gordon, for valuable edits and feedback.

My Mom, for being my final editor and also making me redo the final draft of my fourth grade novel, inspiring decades of carefulness in my work.

Annelise Pruitt, for designing the book cover.

Noah Fecks, for taking my picture.

Summer Smith and Victoria Comella, for cocktail-infused publicity idea sessions.

Anthony Bovino and Edward Clapp, for convincing me that self-publishing would be truest to the artistic mission of this book.

My friends, for supporting me no matter what I do professionally. I'll never be able to repay you for sitting through all my off-off-Broadway plays.

My mentors-from-afar, for inspiring me without even knowing it. I dream of meeting each of you someday.

And everyone I ever worked with artistically, for being part of my journey. Much success to you all – keep pursuing what you truly, uniquely want to do.

About the Author

Ciara Pressler is a former performer in New York City. She is the founder and CEO of Pressler Collaborative, a marketing and communications collective that develops strategy for innovative businesses and creative professionals. Ciara loves marathon running, martinis, and, most of all, helping others identify what they want in their professional lives and determining the actions to make it happen.

Find out more at www.CiaraPressler.com

Made in the USA
Middletown, DE
05 June 2020